IKEBANA

IKEBANA

A PRACTICAL AND PHILOSOPHICAL GUIDE TO JAPANESE FLOWER ARRANGEMENT

STELLA COE

EDITED BY MARY L. STEWART

THE OVERLOOK PRESS

WOODSTOCK · NEW YORK

First published in the United States by
The Overlook Press
Lewis Hollow Road
Woodstock, New York 12498

Library of Congress Cataloging in Publication Data

Coe, Stella
  Ikebana: Japanese flower arrangement.

  Includes index.
  1. Flower arrangement, Japanese— Sōgetsu
school.
I. Stewart, Mary L.   II. Title
SB450.5.S6C63   1984   745.92′252   83–13449
ISBN 0–87951–204–0

This book was designed and produced by John
Calmann and Cooper Ltd, London

Filmset by Keyspools Ltd, Golborne, Lancs, UK
Printed in Hong Kong by Mandarin Offset Ltd

*All the photographs except nos. 1, 3, 7, 8, 9, 11, 12,
71, 75 and 94 were taken by Tim Imrie*

CONTENTS

To my Sogetsu family, of all nationalities
throughout the world

FOREWORD

When I was invited to the Ikebana International First European Regional Conference in 1983, I visited England and met Stella Coe for the first time. I had often heard of her through my father, Sofu, who told me that she is the pioneer teacher of the Sogetsu School in Europe. I was very much impressed by her energy and ability: although over eighty years old, she managed the conference smoothly and with expertise. She was also very kind and gentle to me, a visitor from abroad.

Now Sogetsu students all over the world are full of enthusiasm for the new Sogetsu curriculum, and it is a very good moment to publish this book, which will reinforce the vitality of our art. Stella Coe's many arrangements, which result from her close involvement and keen attachment to ikebana over nearly sixty years, will be a source of inspiration for us.

It is with the greatest appreciation that I celebrate the publication of this book.

Hiroshi Teshigahara
Headmaster
Sogetsu School

1 Arrangement by Hiroshi Teshigahara

INTRODUCTION

Twenty years ago I wrote my first book on ikebana. At that time the only non-Japanese people who knew what the word meant were those who, like me, had lived in Japan and had become familiar with its traditional arts. Ikebana International had only just come into existence six years before (by eastern standards, a very short time), and the London and Washington Chapters of Ikebana International were in their infancy. It seemed appropriate to write a book giving the basic principles of the Sogetsu School of ikebana in order to introduce it to the world of flower arrangers.

Since that time, a number of books have come out in the west as well as in Japan, some of which have been either translated into western languages or written especially for non-Japanese students and followers. My second book, *Free-Style Ikebana*, appeared in 1973. As soon as it was published, it was enthusiastically bought up, for ikebana in general and the Sogetsu School in particular have become increasingly popular. Since then I have often been asked when I was going to write another book. Here is my third on the subject. My aim and hope is that it will fill a need for Sogetsu students and enthusiasts in a number of areas not already met by books in print, as well as setting out in clear terms the principles and practice of the school for beginners.

My involvement with ikebana and the Sogetsu School has spanned more than half my life. I was first introduced to it in my own house, when I was living in Tokyo in the late 1920s. A young member of my household, Seiko Ogawa, would create beautiful flower arrangements out of the most unlikely material. After a while I found that I could not simply watch her work without knowing how she did it. I learned that Miss Ogawa was a qualified teacher of the Sogetsu School, and after initial instruction from her, I enrolled as a student.

In the early days my study was only an interesting pastime, but it quickly became wholly absorbing. For six of the twelve years I lived in Japan, ikebana played a major part in my life. I was then the only foreigner in the school.

2 Tubes of extruded plastic make a striking no-container arrangement with green orchids and fatsia leaves on a black reflecting base (*see p. 99*)

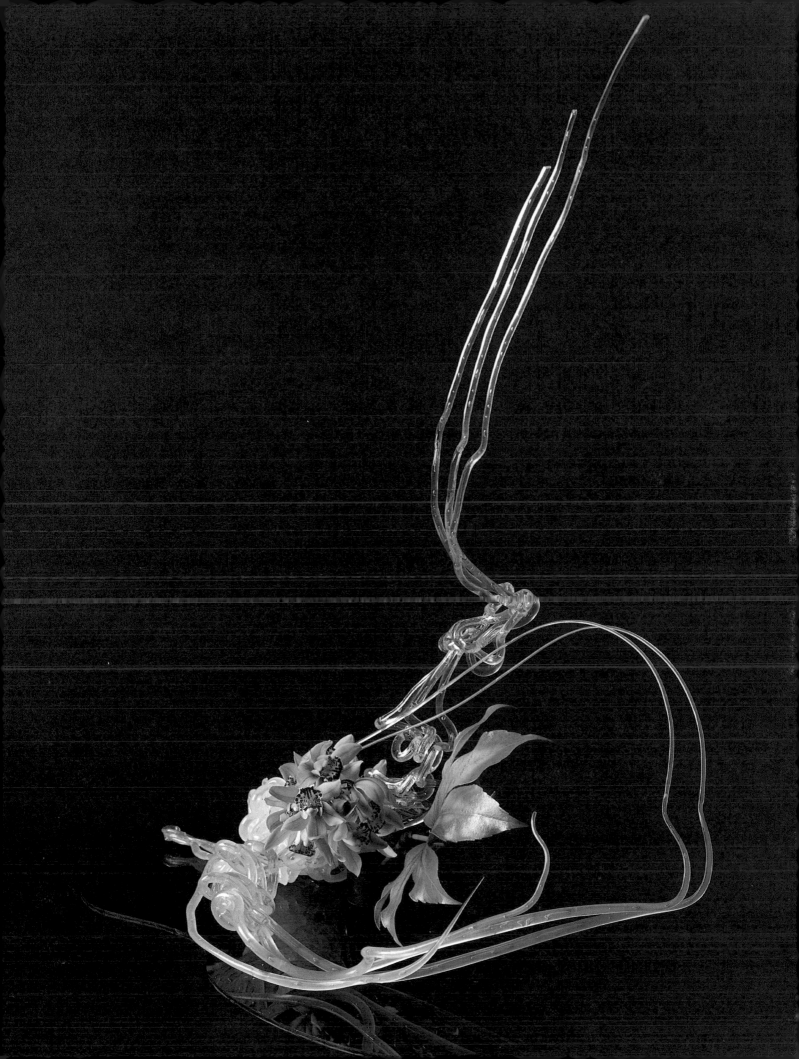

Of the modern schools of ikebana, the Sogetsu School even then was the largest and the best known. I was very fortunate in being able to study with Sofu Teshigahara, its founder. When I left Japan, I continued to practise, giving classes and demonstrations to those who expressed an interest in learning about ikebana.

Since the Second World War I have lived mainly in America and Great Britain, and am now living in London. For over fifty years I have been practising and teaching Sogetsu School ikebana in the west, watching interest in it grow and develop, and promoting that interest where I have been able.

It goes without saying, however, that no art can acquire an international following by virtue of the work of one or even a number of teachers alone. After a time the students themselves discovered a need for an organiz-ation. The history of Ikebana International is by now well known, but it bears repeating, as it has been, and

3 *Far left* Woodblock print by
Katsukawa Shuncho: the *oiran*
Kuniyo of the Yodo-ya watching her
kamaro present a bunch of iris to an
attendant

4 *Left* The lushness of autumn:
breeze blocks with green beech
leaves and dried vine (*see p. 116*)

continues to be, such an integral part of my life.

Ikebana International was the brain-child of Ellen
Gordon Allen, the wife of an American general posted to
Japan. Returning to America after a two-year stay in
Japan, Mrs Allen felt cut off from the world of ikebana in
which she had been active. She discovered that other
enthusiasts in America shared her feeling and welcomed
the idea of forming an association that would maintain
direct contact with ikebana in Japan, as well as linking its
devotees throughout the world. The Grand Masters of the
leading schools in Japan were also very keen for Mrs
Allen's plan to come to fruition. Ikebana International was
born on 17 August 1955 at the Washington Heights Club
in Tokyo. The aims of the new association were:

To stimulate and cultivate the continuous study and
spread of ikebana;

To develop thereby a better understanding of the
Japanese people, and likewise a better understanding
between all nationalities;

To strengthen the friendship between Masters,
teachers and students;

Above all, to stimulate international friendship and
spread goodwill throughout the world.

The motto of Ikebana International became 'Friendship
through Flowers'. My original tutor and good friend, Miss
Ogawa, wrote inviting me to found the first British chapter
of the association in London. With a nucleus of fourteen
or so friends, mainly students of ikebana, I arranged the
inaugural meeting at the Royal Horticultural Society in
1958. To my delight, that first meeting attracted a
hundred new members, and the London Chapter has
gone from strength to strength ever since.

In Britain the spread of interest has been very gratifying.
There are now more than a dozen chapters and countless
study groups, each of which is the basis for a new chapter.
In the USA there are 90 or so chapters, spread throughout
the country. Other chapters have sprung up all over the
world. Members of the London Chapter have sown the
seed of ikebana in France, Holland, Greece, Germany,
Luxembourg, Italy, Northern Ireland, Denmark, Finland,
Malta and Cyprus. World-wide, the chapters number into
the 200s. The far-reaching achievements of Ikebana
International, and the benefits it offers its many members,
now surpass anything Mrs Allen may have dreamed of.
There is hardly any place in the world today where I.I.

5 Turbulence: wisteria vine with anthurium (*see p. 143*)

membership does not act as a passport, so no member or would-be member need feel like a stranger wherever he or she may travel.

In June 1983, it was my great pleasure to act as co-chairman with Takashi Sawano for the first European Regional Conference, held in Maidstone, Kent. Representatives of 29 countries attended the conference, and Hiroshi Teshigahara, son of the founder of the Sogetsu School and its present headmaster, was our guest of honour and graciously agreed to give us a demonstration.

My life is largely divided between I.I. and Sogetsu Branch activities. Each new year brings a flood of opportunities to plan exciting new programmes: visits from Grand Masters, exhibitions, demonstrations. Among the highlights of the past ten years have been three trips to Japan, the last including Peking and Shanghai, and my involvement in many tours to give workshops and demonstrations in the British Isles, America, Bermuda and Malta, among other places.

In America, ikebana has grown immensely in popularity, as a result of the increasing fascination for things eastern, not only material but especially philosophical and religious.

It could be said that ikebana really achieved recognition in Britain when, in 1979, I was awarded the Veitch Memorial Medal by the Royal Horticultural Society. This award is given to anyone who in the opinion of the judges has 'helped in the advancement and improvement of the science and practice of horticulture'. While I do not see ikebana in quite that light, what I felt was important was the fact that it was being publicly recognized. The Society's distinguished president, Lord Aberconway, said that it was most unusual, in a world dominated by men, for a woman to be accorded the highest teaching rank, *Riji*. But Britain is not the nation of hierarchies that Japan is, so I regard the award as a tribute to all those who have shared my devotion to ikebana, for without them it could not have flourished.

These days I do not travel so much, but continue to give classes, for both beginners and advanced students, some of whom are teachers themselves. A number have been coming regularly for a dozen or more years, and consequently we are able to go beyond the immediate concerns of arranging flowers into the philosophical realm.

While the Sogetsu is a modern school of ikebana, it is rooted in the Japanese tradition of developing a special art-form as a discipline of the inner spirit for the ultimate purification of the mind and heart. This transforming, transcending aspect of ikebana is little known to the general public, but it is by no means difficult or obscure. I have found, as have many of my students, that practice in the art of ikebana over the years has significantly deepened my understanding of life, and I have been able to accept its vicissitudes and trials with a tranquillity afforded by no other activity. The correlation between ikebana and this goal is the study of Buddhist principles, specifically those of Zen Buddhism. Like ikebana, Zen Buddhism has been widely and enthusiastically embraced outside Japan, not only in Europe and America but also in Australia and New Zealand. Its popularity likewise demonstrates the way in which a Japanese development meets a universal need, so it is quite natural that Zen and ikebana should be studied simultaneously, and that this combined study be undertaken more widely as students advance in their practice.

It is with this thought in mind that I have decided to write a new book on Sogetsu School ikebana. Since I want it to be used by all grades of students I have not assumed any prior knowledge of the subject. The first chapter

6 Cosmic vitality: striped carnations and hornbeam branches in iridiscent glass containers (*see* p. 139)

discusses the origins of ikebana and the various schools. In the second chapter the tools of the trade are presented and explained. The next three chapters are devoted to the principles and fundamentals of the two basic styles used in Sogetsu School ikebana—*moribana* and *nageire*. Chapters VI and VII are concerned with advanced arrangements, usually called free-style, abstract and avant-garde, and suggest ways of using a wide variety of materials as well as special themes—in this case the four seasons—which an ikebana arrangement can illustrate.

I am not so interested in presenting the most up-to-date arrangements as in encouraging even the less self-confident to make the widest possible use of what may be a very limited selection of materials, such as might be found in the home, garden, local florist or nearby field. The wildly exotic or extravagant is not what I am aiming at, for while an arranger creating such effects may be the centre of attention, he or she is unlikely to penetrate the fabric of life and arrive at an understanding of universal and eternal truths. This leads me to the last chapter of the book, 'Ikebana as a Way of Life'. Here I am introducing a number of Zen themes which have been popular with students, and which seem to be accessible to all Sogetsu School followers. I have also illustrated some ikebana arrangements expressing emotional moods or inspired by poetry, in this case the Japanese 17-syllable verse known as *haiku*. I wish to whet the arranger's appetite and encourage experimentation, set off a new train of thought or activate a new way of looking at materials and thinking up subjects. Those who make arrangements regularly at home may receive fresh inspiration and may develop a more profound understanding of the art.

I would like to thank my friends and fellow teachers who have so kindly consented to assist in the creation of the beautiful and original arrangements presented in this book: Elspeth Pryor, Jean Hixon, Elisabeth Morley, Margaret East and, of course, Mary Stewart. Every one of them unhesitatingly ransacked her garden on the days set aside for photography. I am most grateful to my good friend Elspeth Pryor, who generously offered her house and barn to give us the space necessary to set up the arrangements and photograph them.

I am sorry that it was simply not possible to include the arrangements of other friends who work with me. Often in the studio during our sessions I have wished the

photographer were present, as so many lovely and extraordinary arrangements have appeared, all very different yet all on one and the same theme. My sincere thanks are due to Tim Imrie who took the marvellous photographs: a difficult job done most successfully.

Finally, I would like to extend my grateful thanks to Mary Stewart, as there is no doubt that without her this book would never have been written. She gave me the help and support I needed throughout. She has been of immense value because of her research into the background of ikebana and its relationship to Zen Buddhist teaching. Mary first studied with Margaret East, who, when she was living in Japan, worked with my former teacher, Miss Ogawa. She obtained her teacher's diploma through me. In our mutual study of Buddhist teachings and their influence on all Japanese art, we share the desire to delve further into the mysteries of intuitive acceptance which is necessary for the expression of thoughts and feelings in an ikebana arrangement. This is surely the ultimate aim: to help one another to see the unseen. I am deeply grateful to Mary, not only for her hard work but also for the pleasure and fun we have had working together.

A book on its own is no substitute for study with a qualified teacher. If you are just starting, I encourage you to proceed with your classes and use this book as an accompaniment to your work. If you are an advanced student, refresh your memory with a quick look at the basics, then proceed to try some of the philosophical and poetic arrangements in the later chapters. It is my experience that once you begin to explore these more thought-provoking topics, your ikebana will take on a new dimension.

Stella Coe, VMH
Master (*Riji*)
Sogetsu School

London, 1984

CHAPTER I

THE BACKGROUND OF IKEBANA AND THE SOGETSU SCHOOL

The word *ikebana* is usually translated as 'flower arrangement', and is understood to mean Japanese flower arrangement. But a more accurate interpretation would be 'living plant material' arrangement. It is the art of arranging more than flowers. In fact, the flowers are generally the least important part of an arrangement, unless they are used as the three main lines. I will say more about that in a later chapter. It is important to understand that as ikebana is Japanese, not western, flower arranging, and a Japanese art perfected through centuries of tradition, how you go about it will require a different way of thinking about flowers and about arranging them.

A few of the main differences can be quickly noted. Western arrangements tend to favour a mass of flowers, full-blown flowers playing the predominant part and the combination of colours having the greatest importance. The Japanese approach is just the opposite. You might almost say that the Japanese rule of thumb is: the fewer flowers the better. The full-blown flower, the half-open bud and the tight bud may be used to symbolize past, present and future. The Japanese emphasize the significance of the whole of a flower or branch, its life cycle, so to speak; what you see in a single flower, or any other piece of plant material you may use, can epitomize the eternal processes of the universe. The concern expressed here is not impractical – quite the contrary: by learning to focus your attention on your ikebana in a wider and ultimately deeper context, you come to understand and respect the nature of the material you are working with in the same practical and direct manner as a gardener does.

By the same token, ikebana attaches great importance to the seasons. For this reason I have included in this book a section on seasonal arrangements, which will indicate to you the range and subtlety that it is possible to realize. This again reflects the Japanese understanding of and respect for nature in all its manifold aspects. By using seasonal materials you are in harmony with nature. While it is certainly possible in most places to buy flowers that are out of season, and there is no rule saying you must not

7 Woodblock print by Kuniyasu: devotees of the Buddha argue about offerings (commemorative print for two actors)

use these for a special effect on a particular occasion, or to illustrate a particular point, I always ask the students who come to my studio to bring material from their gardens or from the countryside so that their arrangements, by and large, will be seasonal. In addition to this, there is an economic consideration. Always buying your flowers from the florist can be expensive. Having to look around you for something suitable gives you an appreciation for what you do find, and stimulates your ingenuity and imagination.

Ikebana is, of course, decorative, but decorative in the broader sense I have been talking about, as the symbolic representation of nature. Because the decorative aspect is the end result of practising a time-honoured art, the care

8 Woodblock print by Kunisada: a party of actors, artists and *geisha* admiring an artist's work

taken in planning the arrangement rather than the creation of a big, splashy burst of colour will dictate the ultimate effect. I am not suggesting that it is necessary to change your religion or undergo a radical psychological transformation in order to practise ikebana: I am simply saying that ikebana as a decorative art has a harmonizing, not a punctuating function. The consideration of where your arrangement is to go is therefore just as important as what materials you will use.

Traditionally, the Japanese house is a room which contains no furniture. Cushions and tables are brought out of cupboards when needed and put straight back when not in use. The walls are sliding doors, of paper for the inner walls, glass for the outer ones. There is an alcove on the garden side of the room, known as the *tokonoma*, usually six feet wide and three feet deep, into which an ikebana arrangement would go. On the wall of a *tokonoma* is a hanging scroll picture—a *kakemono*—which is changed with the seasons. Obviously, the arrangement has to harmonize with the picture (especially if it is a painting of flowers), with the season and with the view outside. Harmony does not mean, however, duplicating the material depicted in the painting: if chrysanthemums appear in the *kakemono*, you would be best advised not to use them in your arrangement.

The Japanese are particularly fond of evoking moods or memories and expressing them either in poems or in ikebana arrangements. They think in concrete, visual terms rather than abstract, theoretical ones: by producing something to look at, the arranger aims to activate a whole train of thoughts and feelings. The powers of association that may have influenced an arrangement often seem to strike a similar chord in those who view it. It is the visual impact—the decorative effect, if you will—that starts an emotional response. I regard this reaction, when it comes, as the recognition of a true work of art. The work's spiritual and philosophical intentions need not be apparent, but it is the fact that they are there behind the creation of the arrangement that gives it its vitality.

Once these relatively simple adjustments in thinking have been made, it is not difficult to translate ikebana into a western environment. It is important, however, to place your arrangement against a plain background, for the last thing you want to do is to have it competing with the

9 Woodblock print by Hokusai: a lady preparing sprays of blossom for a pedestal vase

wallpaper. While western arrangements stress colour, ikebana stresses the line, so you must put the arrangement where the lines can be clearly seen. Rather than redecorate, I suggest you purchase a Japanese screen made of wood and paper. This will throw your arrangement into bold relief and will also be completely compatible with your furnishings.

It would be most unusual to meet a Japanese woman who has not studied ikebana, no matter what her social or economic status, as the adornment of her home depends on her skill and ingenuity. Even as the western-style home becomes increasingly prevalent, ikebana is consistently and cleverly adapted to suit the surroundings.

While you may think of ikebana as a largely feminine pursuit, women have taken it up only comparatively recently. Most of the heads and senior teachers of ikebana schools are men, and it is not unusual for a business executive to take it up. Ikebana arrangements are commonplace in many office buildings and factories, where courses may be offered to employees, as well as in hotels, restaurants, department stores, and, of course, temples and shrines. The major department stores in Tokyo have facilities for and often sponsor ikebana exhibitions.

Historically, ikebana has been the pursuit of Buddhist priests, noblemen and *samurai*, or warriors. It has its roots in the native Japanese religion, Shinto, and in the religion imported from Korea, Buddhism. Shinto is, quite simply, reverence for all natural things, which are regarded as homes of spirits. While other cultures have the custom of offering flowers to their gods—the personifications of natural forces—the early Shinto priests took the custom a step further: they offered the entire, living plant, roots and all, not just its blossoms.

With Buddhism came the Korean and Chinese custom of offering flowers to an image of the Buddha. In a sense, ikebana represents a synthesis of the two types of religious offering, the whole plant and the flower. There was no conflict whatsoever in this resolution. It is the genius of the Japanese, in fact, to reconcile apparent conflicts.

The first arrangements were devised in the seventh century by a court noble who retired to the priesthood, Ono-no-Imoko. He had been an envoy to the imperial court of China and had absorbed much of what he had

10 A basic slanting *nageire* arrangement with pine branches and roses (*see p.75*)

seen there. Impressed with the way the Chinese laid out their gardens, upon his return to Japan he built himself a garden after their fashion but with much greater refinement and restraint. Its small lakes and bridges created a fashion and set a pattern which has since become universally accepted as typically Japanese. However, Ono-no-Imoko was less enthusiastic about the way the Chinese Buddhist priests placed their offerings of flowers before the Buddha in a haphazard manner. He decided to find a more fitting means for presenting a floral offering. He retired to his garden, built himself a small house, and devoted the rest of his life to the development of flower arrangement. The task he set himself was typically Japanese in its paradoxical nature. He was trying to find a way to cut the flower (or branch) from its native stem, thereby shortening its life, and then find a way of placing it in water in order to prolong its life. But he went further than that. As a Buddhist priest he felt that an arrangement placed before an image of the Buddha should symbolize the whole universe. From this beginning in a humble hut beside a pond—*ike-no-bo*—came the style known as *rikka*, 'standing up plant cuttings'. For hundreds of years the techniques were passed from master to master, usually priests.

In fact the early *rikka* were, according to wood-block prints we have of them, enormous. Some could be twelve, fifteen or even twenty feet in height and would take weeks to construct. The flowers and branch tips all pointed towards heaven. This style was well suited to the spaciousness of temples—and eventually palaces, for the nobles began to take up the art—and the time and trouble involved in creating an arrangement were in keeping with its religious significance. For any other purpose it would have been completely impractical, but at that time no other purpose was envisaged. For many centuries, therefore, ikebana was to remain the prerogative of priests and noblemen.

During its formative years, the *ikenobo* art produced many brilliant exponents, but none so illustrious as a fifteenth-century priest known as Senkei Ikenobo. Such was the flow of pilgrims to his temple in Kyoto that his fame rapidly spread and he founded his own school of flower arrangement. This was the beginning of the Ikenobo school, which had its origin in the seventh century and is flourishing today.

It was natural, of course, that as the art of ikebana spread and developed, more practical dimensions should evolve. This is precisely what happened in the eleventh century when military rule replaced the authority of the court. At that time, the military ruler or *shogun*, Yorimoto, chose the strict and simple meditational form of Buddhism known in Japan as Zen for his warrior way of life. In Zen practice there is no room for enormous images of Buddhas, let alone elaborate *rikka*, or formal, arrangements. But ikebana was recognized, along with other arts, as a means of calming and purifying the mind; it was therefore adapted to the training needs of the *samurai* and practised by them as a means of composing their minds in order to be at one with nature, to experience neither hesitation nor fear.

The *tokonoma* was erected as the quiet place in a *samurai*'s house where he could meditate and study. He might create an arrangement, a single flower or branch in a tall vase—a style that came to be called *nageire*, or 'thrown-in', and which dates from the twelfth century—or paint a landscape or practise calligraphy whilst sitting in the *tokonoma*. The painting might be mounted and hung on the wall, and the ikebana placed by it along with an incense burner.

The evolution of the tea ceremony, also a meditational practice, created the need for the tea house with the *tokonoma* as an integral but purely decorative part, and the need for a *chabana*, a small, natural arrangement suitable to the simplicity and starkness of the ceremony. It is said that the celebrated tea and ikebana master, Senko-Rikyu, created the *nageire* style. And the first book on ikebana dates from this time, the *Sendenshō*. Written by another tea and flower master, Ippo, it explains how to arrange flowers for special occasions in accordance with the seasons. The terms *shin*, referring to the main branch in an arrangement, and *soe*, referring to the secondary branch, appear in this book.

Whereas the *rikka* and its modified form *seika* (a symbolic triad of heaven, man and earth) were designed for very complicated Buddhist rituals and court rites, the styles influenced by Zen represent the unity of nature and bring natural objects into the home as decorative additions. Their first aim remained religious as they symbolized the unity of all things and provided composure and tranquillity for the arranger as well as the viewer.

Both styles were popular and continued to be practised in the many different schools of ikebana that sprang up over the centuries.

With the gradual emergence of the merchant class from the seventeenth century onwards, ikebana underwent a variety of refinements and was taken up by the Japanese as a whole, as part of their cultural inheritance. These refinements, which also took place in many other arts, developed in isolation: for over two centuries the rulers of Japan decided to prevent all foreigners from living in or even visiting their country. When as a result of Commodore Perry's gunboat diplomacy in 1854 Japan again opened its doors, western influences began to produce the same dramatic transformations as had Chinese influences in the past. Quickly they were met and absorbed, giving rise to new schools and modifications in the old schools to suit the demands of a modern population. A new style, *moribana*, 'piled-up flowers' in a shallow container, usually ceramic, appeared. Ikebana arrangers began using western flowers. The *kenzan*, or pinholder, came into being.

Of the popular schools, Enshu dates from the sixteenth century, Koryu from the eighteenth. Of the newer schools, Ohara was founded in the 1890s, and the Sogetsu-ryu, or School of the Grass Moon, in the 1920s.

There are many schools, of course, and the one I am teaching is Sogetsu. It has a wide following both in and outside Japan, possibly because it is the most easily translated into the language of other cultures. Sofu Teshigahara, the founder of the Sogetsu School, said that Sogetsu brings out the individuality of each arranger. The student follows basic principles, to be sure, but according to his or her own understanding and choice of materials and containers. The individual personality is not entirely lost. Such a statement was revolutionary in a time before most contemporary schools developed their own abstract and free-style forms. Sofu Teshigahara started studying ikebana at the age of six with his father, a famous teacher of classical styles. He broke with established tradition in his early twenties and founded his own school, based on the modern styles of *nageire* and *moribana* but going beyond them into free-style, abstract and avant-garde experiments. Sofu Teshigahara had an international reputation, and has been called the Picasso of ikebana in recognition of his imaginative and inventive genius.

11 Arrangement by Sofu
Teshigahara, founder of the Sogetsu
School

At his death in 1979, he was succeeded by his daughter Kasumi, herself an imaginative and delicate abstract exponent. Following her tragic death a year later, her brother, Hiroshi, became the headmaster of the school. He comes to flower-arranging with a background in films and ceramics, so presenting innovative challenges to Sogetsu exponents throughout the world. On a recent visit to England he demonstrated some of his new ideas to one hundred Sogetsu teachers. These included designing with paper and using paper in an arrangement in order to give a more vividly three-dimensional effect. Although he is anxious to provide new direction to the school, he is

12 Basket arrangement by Kasumi
Teshigahara

equally anxious to uphold its traditions. I am looking forward with great fascination to see just how these new ideas are received and expressed by Sogetsu enthusiasts.

One thing has remained constant throughout the growth of ikebana and that is its symbolism. Its present-day application is explained in Chapter 3, where it is an essential part of the definition of the three main placements used in arrangements. Suffice it to say that this symbolism is the very root of ikebana, and is thus the crucial differentiating factor between Japanese and western flower-arranging.

The basic principles and the basic arrangements given in this book are those of the Sogetsu School. They are intended only as a guide. That is, they will not tell you what you will finally do in practising your ikebana. You are not meant to copy, branch by branch, flower by flower, what you have been shown here. The art of ikebana is highly original, as Sofu Teshigahara himself has said. But every art has a foundation, and only after you have a firm and confident grasp on that foundation will your imagination take wing. It is therefore essential that the principles be carefully studied. The keynote to success is practice: only constant practice will lead to perfection. On the way, however, I can assure you of many happy and richly rewarding hours.

CHAPTER II

MATERIALS, CONTAINERS AND TOOLS

Having given you something of the historical background to ikebana and the Sogetsu School, I want now to acquaint you with the materials, containers and tools you will be most likely to use.

In a sense little short of an encyclopaedia of all growing plant-life would be adequate here, for in ikebana, your choice of material is virtually limitless. You do not need a degree in horticulture, however, to discover what you do need. And the Latin name of any plant material is of no consequence. If a flower or a branch or a plant looks right to you, use it. You are sure to learn the horticultural names of various plants eventually, from knowing friends if nothing else, and this knowledge will only add to your understanding of your material, but it is by no means crucial.

Useful material for ikebana can be found in the highways and byways. Beginners will soon find that their eyes are fully opened to the possibilities in nature. Mosses, roots, leaves, lichen-covered branches, oak-apples, fungus, are all of use and you will quickly develop the habit of keeping a lookout. The consequence of this constant seeking is a tremendous interest in all growing things. There are many pleasurable discoveries to be made about things you are forever seeing without really noticing. Were you aware, for instance, that the tips of all growing branches turn up towards the sun? Even a branch with a strong downward curve has an upward-turning tip. It is this striving towards the sun that gives the branch its look of life and vigour.

I will not list the many unlikely-seeming items that can be incorporated into arrangements. As you develop an eye for line and shape you will soon learn to make your own discoveries, which is far more exciting than being told what to look for.

Apart from scouring the countryside or your garden for likely material it is always worth trying your local florist. With the ever-growing interest in it, some florists are beginning to cater for those who do Japanese flower-arranging. They stock a variety of curved branches and

13 Woodblock print by Toyokuni: a lady making an arrangement of plum branches

are not at all taken aback at being asked for just two or three flowers rather than a bunch. My own feeling is that once a demand has been established the florists will be only too happy to cater for it, so do not hesitate to make your requirements known.

Since almost anything can be used in ikebana, however, you should not have difficulty in finding *some* branch, leaf or root with which to practise arrangements. It is not the type of material chosen but the use to which it is put that matters. What is of real importance is that your flowers should look their best and be given the longest possible chance of survival. There is no virtue in devising a brilliant arrangement with flowers that have not received proper care and attention. Whether the arrangement be simple or spectacular it will be rendered completely ineffective if the flowers look dull and lifeless. It is therefore necessary to know how to treat your flowers before you start to arrange them.

FLOWER CARE

If you are going to take flowers from your garden, they should be cut either in the early morning or the early evening. It is at these times that the stems will be filled with a life-giving flow of moisture that should be re-established as quickly as possible if your flowers are to last. To ensure this, you need to have with you a small bucket of water in which to place each flower the moment it has been cut. By so simple an operation you will have taken the most vital step in prolonging the life of your material.

Once in the house the stems should be cut again, under water, near the base and on the diagonal, before being stood in water until you are ready to use them. The diagonal cut makes sure that the stems will not stand square to the bottom of the container and choke off the intake of water. It is not possible to over-emphasize the importance of a continuous supply of water to your flowers, and the point to bear in mind is that *the cutting of stems should always take place in water*. If you hold the flower in the air while cutting its stem then it immediately begins to lose its strength. Be sure to have a bowl of water handy and hold each flower so that its stem is in the water while you are making the diagonal cut.

Flowers bought from the florist require exactly the same treatment as soon as you get them home: the diagonal cut, *in water.*

There are some flowers, of course, that require rather more encouragement than a mere drink of cold water. If you are a gardener you will undoubtedly know about these; if not, your florist will be able to advise you. In general, though, flowers whose stems have a stickiness about them when they are cut, such as poppies and tulips, are given their best chance of long life if they are stood in boiling water for a few minutes. Before you give them this heat treatment, wrap the blooms in paper to safeguard them from steam damage.

With the proper care you can be sure that your flowers will be in excellent condition when you are ready to use them, and will last well in the arrangement.

CONTAINERS

In defining what constitutes a container I need make but one stipulation: it must be able to hold at least three inches (about 8 cm) of water. All sorts of objects besides the customary bowls and vases can be used in interesting ways, but never indiscriminately. For, wide as the choice may be, the container must not be regarded as a separate entity. It is an integral part of any arrangement and should never be used simply because it is an attractive colour or has an unusual shape. The container must always be in harmony with the arrangement and should never detract from the flowers.

It is of great importance that containers be kept absolutely clean. They should be thoroughly washed and rinsed when not in use. Dirty containers will pollute the water and quickly cause your flowers to deteriorate.

Beginners are best advised to stick to the conventional types of containers—bowls and vases, quite plain and in undistracting earthy colours such as browns and greens. There is plenty of time to experiment later.

Like flowers, containers can be considered seasonal. This is because certain wares enhance the look of certain flowers. Winter arrangements are seen to their best advantage in metal containers, spring and autumn flowers need pottery to set them off properly, and summer flowers are ideally suited to baskets. This order was once strictly adhered to in Japan, but nowadays it is not too rigidly observed. It does, however, provide a useful guide.

The legend of how baskets came to be used as containers is worth telling. It is said that long ago a Japanese noble was riding in the country and came to a humble farmhouse, where he stopped for tea and asked the farmer to make him a flower arrangement. The poor old farmer, overawed by the splendour of his visitor, was in despair. He had no costly containers and no equipment, but he had to show courtesy to the nobleman. In desperation, he took an ordinary small basket, picked some simple wild flowers and did his best by arranging them with no attempt at flamboyance. When he had done, and having no elaborate stand on which to place the basket, he stood it on the bare earth before his guest. The natural charm of the arrangement delighted the nobleman, and he thereupon decreed that all basket arrangements should be so simple and so beautiful that they would need no further enhancement. And from that time basket arrangements were not required to stand on a decorative base.

BASES

With Japanese flower arrangements it is customary, but not obligatory, to place a base, or *dai*, beneath a vase or bowl. Not only does this provide the finishing touch to an arrangement but it has the practical purpose of protecting the surface beneath.

In Japan the *dai* is usually very special and costly. For as Westerners put their money into furniture and furnishings, so the Japanese will spare no expense for a beautiful and unusual wood with which to adorn further the traditional *tokonoma*. We, too, should want to complement an arrangement by standing the container on an attractive base – but it does not have to be expensive. It might be of wood, lacquer, strips of bamboo strung together, or even a slice of a tree trunk, either polished or in its natural state. The shape of the base will be dictated by the type of container used. A square or rectangular container requires a base that is circular or irregular in shape, while a round container will need a square or rectangular base. The placement of the base can follow the contours of the container but it is infinitely more interesting if it is set at an angle to it. And you will have

14 A selection of containers

noted that a base is usually placed under all containers except baskets.

TOOLS

In some of the big department stores or shops specializing in things Japanese, it is now possible to buy Japanese tool sets consisting of a pair of scissors, a saw, a very small chopper, a two-edged knife and a syringe. They come in a decorative case and are, of course, very useful to have. But they are not essential for Sogetsu School arrangements as long as you have a pair of good scissors. My own preference is for the *hasami* (Japanese scissors), which are quite different from secateurs and much more restful to use. They have no spring and therefore remain closed until you use them. If you cannot obtain these, however, just make sure that your scissors are strong without being unwieldy and that they have a really sharp cutting edge.

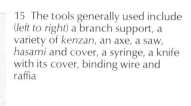

15 The tools generally used include (*left to right*) a branch support, a variety of *kenzan*, an axe, a saw, *hasami* and cover, a syringe, a knife with its cover, binding wire and raffia

THE KENZAN

The *kenzan* or pinholder is your one indispensable piece of equipment in all Sogetsu School shallow-container arrangements, for it is the only means of securing the material.

There are various sizes and types of *kenzan* available, some with the pins set close together and others with the pins more widely spaced. Your particular need will be dictated by the scope of your arrangement and the material used. It is advisable, therefore, to build up a stock of them in different sizes. In doing so, be sure to buy the ones which have heavy lead bases. The lighter types of pinholder used in some Western arrangements are quite unsuitable for ikebana. Remember that those you use must be capable of bearing the weight of branches.

Should a branch prove so heavy that it tips the *kenzan* when put in at the required angle, a second *kenzan* can be placed upside down on the first to counter the weight of the branch. But no artificial aids may be employed to make the *kenzan* adhere to the bottom of the container. The reason for this is that it might be necessary to alter the position of a finished arrangement slightly in the container

in order to improve its overall appearance. If a *kenzan* should slip a little in the container, two thicknesses of newspaper cut to the dimensions of the *kenzan* and placed beneath it will remedy the fault.

WELL KENZAN

This is a *kenzan* in a small metal or bamboo water container. It is employed in basket arrangements and in conjunction with any unorthodox container that will not hold water.

Where no container at all is used—that is, for an arrangement done perhaps in driftwood or directly on to a table—the well *kenzan* is invaluable. And it is small enough to be easily concealed in the finished arrangement.

CUTTING

The preliminaries to doing a flower arrangement are every bit as important as the arrangement itself. Good results are dependent upon proper methods, so the cutting of material cannot be a haphazard affair. It is not just a matter of getting branches and flowers down to the required length. They must be cut in such a way that they can be firmly fixed in the *kenzan*.

Branches are always cut diagonally, the direction of the cut being governed by the part the branch is going to play in your arrangement. That is to say, if the branch is going to curve to the left, as you face it, the cut will be made so that the cut surface of the branch will be to the right. When it is placed in the *kenzan*, then, the pin will pierce the shorter side while the thick part of the branch will rest against the pin, counterbalancing the weight of the branch. Conversely, if the branch curves to the right then the shorter side will be on the left. It is not really as complicated as it sounds, and can be reduced to a formula: whichever direction your branch is to follow, the cut is always made so that the exposed part is uppermost.

A very heavy branch will require a little more attention. After you have made your diagonal cut, slit it up the centre to a maximum of three inches (about 8 cm) from the base. This will allow the water easier access to the entire stem.

Should a branch prove too thin to be effectively secured in the *kenzan*, a leaf wrapped around the part of the stem that is to be impaled will make up the deficiency.

Flowers, at this stage, are not cut diagonally, but straight across the stem, with the stem once again in water at the time of cutting. Most flower stems are comparatively thin and it is not always easy to fix them firmly on the pins of the *kenzan*. To cut them diagonally would be to weaken them further at a point where strength is an advantage.

But even flowers with the thinnest of stems can, with a little ingenuity, be safely used. All you have to do is cut a piece of stem from a thicker-stemmed flower and insert the thin stem into it. About half or three-quarters of an inch (1 or 2 cm) of thick stem will be ample – just enough to hold the thin stem securely in the *kenzan*.

Fig. 1 The correct way to cut flower stems under water for your actual arrangement

TRIMMING

It will be very rare to come across material for an arrangement that does not need a certain amount of trimming. Whether you have an arrangement in mind and are looking for a particular branch, or whether you see an attractive branch that inspires an arrangement, there is bound to be some cleaning up to do.

When you take a branch from a tree you will naturally choose one most closely following the line you think you would like. At first, however, it might seem difficult to discern that line. The off-shoots and foliage could very well confuse your judgement. Being readily able to choose the right branch comes with experience. After you have been working for a while with such material, you will find it quite easy to visualize at a glance the bare outline of a branch. And you will know more or less how much trimming is going to be necessary.

Cutting a branch to scale can also be rather confusing at first. Seen in its natural state, growing in the open, it might appear to be exactly right for your purpose. Taken into the confines of a room, however, it can look surprisingly different. It is all a matter of perspective – and you will develop an eye for it with practice.

For the beginner it is enough to take any branch and study it well, without hurry, until a useful line can be clearly seen. To help determine the line, it is best to fix the

Fig. 2 A branch before trimming, and after trimming to bring out the line

branch in the *kenzan* to do the trimming while it is in position. Once the line is decided upon, it is simply a matter of cutting away all the twigs and leaves that interfere with that particular line. It is especially important to remove anything that is hanging down or has a drooping appearance. The last thing you want is for the branch to look as if it is going to die. When it is trimmed it should have an alert, alive look.

Eventually you will be able to do the trimming before positioning the branch in the *kenzan*. As with all else in flower-arranging, that comes with practice.

Flowers, too, need to be trimmed before they are used in an arrangement. It is essential that the part of the stem that will be below the water level should be absolutely free of buds and leaves. Anything of this nature left on the stem will speedily decay and pollute the water, endangering not only the flowers but the entire arrangement.

BENDING

If it were a matter of waiting to find a branch with exactly the right curve your arrangements might be few and far between. Fortunately, however, the acquiring of just the curve you want presents no great problem. A branch can be bent to your requirements by the following method.

Hold the branch in both hands—the fingers of one hand over the branch and the fingers of the other under it, so that the thumbs are opposite each other—and carefully massage the stem by pressing the thumbs towards each other. Keep the hands moving gradually along the stem, with the thumbs always relative to each other, for to concentrate on a particular part or on a joint is to invite the branch to snap. As a further precaution against snapping, keep twisting the branch slightly as you move your hands along it. Provided pressure is applied gently and evenly, there is no reason why you should not achieve the desired curve.

It goes without saying that the branch you are going to bend must have sap in it. A dry branch will immediately snap if bending is attempted.

You might, while bending a branch, hear a cracking sound without seeing any actual damage. That will be the fibres inside the branch breaking, making the bending that much easier. Only the very experienced—or the extremely lucky novice—can accomplish this without snapping the branch.

In the ordinary course of events you should have no difficulty in bending material if you bear in mind that it is not a job to be rushed. Do not attempt it when your mind is occupied with half a dozen other things. Rather than spoil your material, leave it until you can really take your time.

And by the same token, do not be daunted by a very stubborn branch. Even the toughest will yield if you bend it under water. You can bend a branch most easily under warm water.

Fig. 3 The right way to bend a branch, with even pressure of the thumbs to guard against snapping

I have already mentioned the importance of doing the best for your flowers if you want them to do their best for you. There is, however, still something to be taken into account. It applies just as much to finished arrangements as it does to flowers waiting to be used.

To help them survive for their longest possible span, do not let your flowers stand in a very warm place or in a position where the wind can reach them. Both excessive heat and strong draughts can prove disastrous, as they dry up the moisture in the entire arrangement. In this respect, strong sunlight can be every bit as dangerous as a radiator or other forms of room heating.

CHAPTER III

THE BASIC PRINCIPLES OF THE FUNDAMENTAL STYLES

Mastering the basic principles is necessary for any art-form you might take up, whether western or eastern. Although the terminology and the principles of Sogetsu School ikebana are Japanese, the aim is the same – to understand what you are doing and why you are doing it in a particular way. At first you must simply follow instructions. Your teacher will provide those in abundance, and will certainly answer questions. But only with continuous practice will any of the principles begin to make sense. You must not be discouraged if you are not a master overnight. Persevere, and gradually your intuition will begin to tune in to what you are learning.

There are two fundamental styles of arrangement in the Sogetsu School, each having its guiding principles – and I say 'guiding' advisedly. The joy of flower-arranging is its challenge to the creative ability – and the Sogetsu School was formed, as we have seen, to encourage the greatest possible freedom. So the basic principles are not meant to be restraining bonds, but rather pointers or, if you like, foundation-stones upon which your imagination will build.

The fundamental styles are called *moribana* and *nageire* – *moribana* covering all arrangements done in low, shallow containers and *nageire* those in tall, upright containers. Chapters IV and V cover these in detail. *Moribana* is also known as the natural style because it often depicts a little scene, the branches representing trees and the flowers appearing to grow beneath them. It stresses the pictorial rather than the design element in Japanese flower arrangement.

Moribana containers, whether round, oblong or irregular in shape, should be at least three inches (about 8 cm) deep, thus ensuring that they can hold sufficient water to sustain the material. Ideally, they should be from fourteen to eighteen inches in width (35 to 45 cm).

In all *moribana* arrangements the *kenzan* is used to secure the material. It can be placed to either side of the container, to the front or to the back, but never in the centre. Its position will be determined by the nature of

16 Basic *moribana*: *risshin-kei* No. 4 with willow and water-lilies (*see p. 59*)

Fig. 4 Positioning stems in the *kenzan*

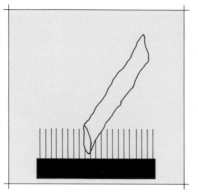

your arrangement. For one that sweeps towards the left the *kenzan* will have to be either to the front or back of the right-hand side of the container, and vice versa.

The reason for avoiding the centre of the container is a natural one. Nothing in nature is exactly symmetrical, say the Japanese, and consequently they do not want symmetry in their arrangements. Anything perfectly balanced has no movement, and anything absolutely still appears dead. All arrangements must have the appearance of living and growing—so, as in nature, absolute symmetry may be approached but never reached.

FIXING MATERIAL IN THE KENZAN

Since the firm fixing of material in the *kenzan* is one of the fundamentals of the *moribana* style, it is important that it should be done with skill and care. The *kenzan* is not as formidable as it may at first appear, and plenty of practice with any bits of branch will soon give you the feel of it. Skill will come with practice.

The method of fixing branches is to press them down firmly in a vertical position on to the pins and then tilt them in the required direction—remembering, of course, that the cut edge of the stem will be uppermost.

Flowers are inserted at their desired angles with enough pressure to ensure that the stems are pierced by the pins.

It is the simplicity of working with the *kenzan* that makes *moribana* arrangements the easiest to do.

MAIN PLACEMENTS

So far I have talked about branches generally, but now it is time to look at them individually.

Every flower arrangement has its main placements, which govern the overall height and width of the arrangement. Once they have been placed in position everything added comes within their scope and never extends beyond the limits they impose. But to the Japanese they are more than just a framework: they have their special names and special meanings. Not all the Japanese schools call them by the same names, but all the names used have the same basic significance.

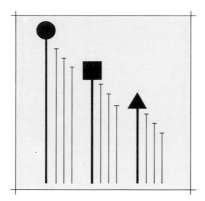

Fig. 5 The proportions of the three main placements, with *jushi* in relation to each

There are three main placements, and they are common to both *moribana* and *nageire* arrangements. In the Sogetsu School they are known as *shin* (heaven), *soe* (man) and *hikae* (earth), names illustrating the inherent symbolism of Japanese flower arrangement. It might be more comprehensible to a western arranger if we give these words their deeper interpretation—spiritual truth, harmonizer and material substance. The significance is that man, in his flower-arranging, is supposed to harmonize spiritual truth with material substance.

It is important to remember that oriental artists never study merely for art's sake. Whatever they do is really a striving to gain enlightenment. If a painting ends up as merely a pretty picture it is not considered worth the doing, and a flower arrangement should be something more than just a decoration for the home. With the whole of the universe represented in the three main stems, the Japanese flower arranger has limitless inspiration for creative effort: the result should invite study and contemplation.

This might seem irrelevant at this stage, but I cannot emphasize too strongly that to become really proficient in your art your approach should be akin to that of the Japanese.

Of the three main placements, *shin* is the longest and most important line, *soe* is the medium line, and *hikae* is the shortest line. Other material is added only after these three are in position.

Additional branches and flowers are called *jushi* and they may be used to supplement any or all of the main placements. There is no limit to the number that can be used in one arrangement, provided that you work in odd numbers—one, three, five, seven and so on. As with the placing of the *kenzan*, it is a question of avoiding symmetry. Even numbers suggest perfect balance, so they are not encouraged.

Jushi are always shorter than the main stem they supplement—and they are never as long as each other. They must always be cut to varying lengths. It can be appreciated that a number of flowers of exactly the same length would give an arrangement a dull, heavy and completely unnatural look.

To begin with, it would be best to keep your tallest supplementary flower down to about two thirds the length of the main stem.

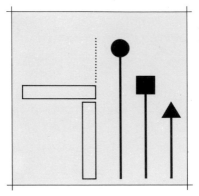

Fig. 6 Standard *moribana* measurements

MEASUREMENTS FOR MAIN PLACEMENTS

There must always be a sense of proportion between an arrangement and its container. It hardly needs to be said that a large arrangement in a tiny container or a small arrangement in a huge container will look ridiculous. The lengths of the main placements, therefore, are dependent on the size of the container and can be determined in the following way.

STANDARD-SIZED ARRANGEMENTS
Shin is equivalent to the width of the container plus the depth and up to half as much again.
Soe is three-quarters of *shin*.
Hikae is three-quarters of *soe*.
(Standard proportions are used in all diagrams and style descriptions.)

LARGE ARRANGEMENTS
Shin is equivalent to twice the sum of the width of the container plus the depth.
Soe is three-quarters of *shin*.
Hikae is half of *soe*.

SMALL ARRANGEMENTS
Shin is equivalent to the width of the container plus the depth.
Soe is three-quarters of *shin*.
Hikae is three-quarters of *soe*.

All of the foregoing measurements are applicable to both *moribana* and *nageire* arrangements. In the case of *nageire*, however, they are intended to indicate the length of the placement above the rim of the container. This means that for *nageire* you must allow a little more to account for the amount of stem that will actually be inside the container.

Bear in mind that the measurements are not hard and fast rules but only guides.

POSITIONING OF PLACEMENTS

In all the basic arrangements and their variations the three main stems are placed at certain angles, and there is a guide to these, too. The angles used are 10°, 45° and 75° and they are measured from the upright zero, which is an imaginary line rising vertically from the point where the *shin* branch is put into the *kenzan*. It is the tips of the main branches—this is most important—that must be at the given angles from the upright zero. The branches are interchangeable at these angles, depending on the requirements of the arrangement sought or the effect required. And provided that the tips maintain their angles they can face anywhere in their respective planes—that is, within a radius of 180°.

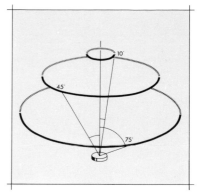

Fig. 7 The angles and directional scope for your material

Figure 7 illustrates what I mean. It shows the wide scope available within the prescribed angles. The circumferences of the three circles are variously at 10°, 45° and 75° from the upright zero, so that the tip of a main branch could touch any point on the front half of one of the circles. Since the majority of arrangements were originally to be viewed from the front only, you will not yet be concerned with the 180° indicated by a dotted line.

An ideal arrangement would have the tips of the main stems pointing to one another so that the eye of the viewer is drawn to the centre or heart of the arrangement—which is where the *jushi* would be. But no *moribana* arrangement would be considered anything like ideal if the *kenzan*, or any part of it, were visible from the correct viewing distance of three feet (1 m) in front of the arrangement. It is essential that it should be camouflaged, and in a way that is in keeping with the overall picture. The addition of leaves at the base of the arrangement will often take care of this, at the same time giving weight to the whole structure. Visual weight is needed to give the feeling of branches and flowers growing from the earth.

Normally you will look at an arrangement from the front, but you are also looking through it, as you would a natural scene, so in these arrangements you want to avoid a flat appearance. In fact, every Japanese flower arrangement must have a three-dimensional look. It is for this reason that all material should incline towards the front. This will create the illusion of depth.

It is put more attractively by the Japanese. They say that the front of the arrangement is the south and the back is the north. Since the south is nearest to the sun, the branches and flowers—as in nature—will be reaching forward and upwards towards the sun. In the north—the back of the arrangement—where very little grows, there will be only undeveloped material or pieces that are not very good.

This I consider to be a very helpful picture for beginners. Think of yourself as the sun, with everything reaching out and up towards you, and you will not go wrong.

THE PERSONAL ELEMENT

The state of mind of the arranger is considered by the Japanese to be more important than the arrangement, and it is said that one should never start out to make a flower arrangement when mentally confused. I would amend that view slightly: if you are upset about something, getting yourself ready to make an arrangement can be a good way to calm the mind. It is a good idea to sit quietly for a while if you have travelled any distance to the place where you will do your arranging. You need to relax and compose yourself. Collecting your material, cutting and trimming the branches, planning the arrangement all have a tranquillizing effect on your mind. The pressures of modern life mean that you are unlikely to find many periods of absolute peace, so you have to make a conscious attempt to calm down before you can start creating something beautiful.

Ikebana can actually help us express all facets of the personality—all the moods and temperaments, as you will see later in this book. What is important is that you make the effort to begin, and in making the effort you will find yourself relaxing and forgetting some of your other worries. It is difficult, if not impossible, to start to organize and plan an ikebana arrangement and be worried at the same time. Even if the arrangement is going to express anger or anxiety, the arranger needs to be as calm as possible. The aim is to give the viewer a feeling of repose (even if anger is depicted) and a desire for contemplation. So try to make each step in the creation of your arrangement with your full attention. You are not engaged in a race against time in this pursuit.

No matter what your frame of mind, it is a good plan to collect yourself before you begin. Allow yourself plenty of time, and always work in a way that is most comfortable for you. Sometimes you may like to sit; at other times you may find that you work better standing. I prefer to stand because I find that I am constantly stepping back to look at my work, but it really depends on the type of arrangement I am working on.

It is a good thing, of course, to step back every now and then and view your arrangement in perspective through its various stages. You cannot have a clear idea of its effect if you stay close to it all the time.

Like a painting, a basic flower arrangement should properly be viewed from only one point—directly in front, and at a distance of not less than three feet (1 m). It is seen to its best advantage if it stands just below eye-level. You would sit down, therefore, to study an arrangement in a low position and stand to look at one higher up.

Wherever possible, make your arrangement in the place where it is to stand. If you make it in one place and then move it to another you will invariably have to adjust it slightly so that it accords with its new surroundings.

I have said before that the feel of the material you are using will come with practice. As you grow accustomed to it so you will come closer to the Japanese concept of sublimating self to the arrangement: the difference between forcing a branch the way you think it should go and letting the branch, by its shape and nature, suggest how best it might be employed. As Japanese philosophy has it, you cannot dictate to nature. The only alternative is to put yourself in the secondary position and let nature dictate to you. When this happens you are truly on the road to successful arranging.

Striving for an effect can be disastrous. What you end up with will look contrived and artificial. My own experience has taught me that. Your experience will show you as well that trying to be clever defeats the objective. You need to let your intuition rather than your ego (that is, your pride, desire to show off, to compete with others) determine how you progress. Paradoxically, you will find that in order to progress you need to regress to the basics. Then you will come upon the answer. The principles of the fundamental styles should really become automatic so that you instinctively know when something is wrong and also what to do to make it right. You have to let the material suggest how you should use it.

BASIC FORMS

A brief word is necessary about the two basic forms of the Sogetsu School. These are the *risshin-kei* (basic upright) and the *keishin-kei* (basic slanting) styles, and they are common to both *moribana* and *nageire* arrangements. They are, in fact, just what their names suggest. In the *risshin-kei* style the *shin* stands upright, and no matter what angles are taken by the material the overall appearance of the arrangement is upright. Similarly, in the *keishin-kei* style the *shin* is at an angle, and even if all the other material were upright the overall appearance of the arrangement would be slanting.

USE OF ENGLISH AND JAPANESE TERMS

Throughout this book, I have given both English and Japanese terms used in Sogetsu ikebana. When I was studying in Japan many years ago, only the Japanese terms were used. But then I was the only foreign student in the school. Nowadays the Japanese use the English terms for foreign students. I feel it is important for you to know the original terms so that you will not be at a loss if you should pick up an older book on ikebana. I have also included a glossary in the back of the book for further clarity.

KEY TO DIAGRAMS

In the following pages, each arrangement described is accompanied by a diagram showing the positioning of the main stems. There is also a diagram explaining each basic arrangement and a photograph of each finished basic arrangement. The diagram will clarify exactly how the main branches and flowers have been inserted to gain a particular effect, because it is not always easy to tell from a photograph what the precise positions are. In diagrammatic representation the following signs are used to indicate the main stems:

● shin   ■ soe   ▲ hikae

In the next two chapters you will find instructions for the basic *moribana* and *nageire* styles. These should be studied with a qualified teacher, not simply by this book – or any book. A book is a two-dimensional medium whereas ikebana is so definitely three-dimensional. But if you are studying or have studied with a qualified Sogetsu teacher, you can consult this book as you go along, to help you develop further. It is constant practice that is the real key to success.

CHAPTER IV

BASIC MORIBANA ARRANGEMENTS

Moribana arrangements look their best on a low table against a plain background. And it is not only the background that should be plain. The table, ledge or shelf on which an arrangement stands should be absolutely free of clutter—no ashtrays, no cigarette boxes, nothing at all must be allowed to distract from the arrangement.

The arrangements outlined here can be made with any material. The suggestions for material which preface each one are intended purely as a guide. To attain perfection, every arrangement needs to be practised many times and it is a good plan to vary your material as often as you can. It is surprising, and illuminating, to discover the quite dissimilar effects you will get by doing the same form of arrangement several times, using different material.

In Japan nowadays the basic arrangements are taught with *shin* and *soe* of one material and *hikae* of another. I have found, however, that beginners pick up the rudiments more easily when they use the same material for their three main lines. I suggest that you do this to start with as it will give you a clearer picture of what you are doing, and it does not interfere with the basic issue, which is mastering the techniques of Japanese flower arrangement. But you can make up your own mind about this.

The basic *moribana* styles are as follows.

RISSHIN-KEI (BASIC UPRIGHT STYLE)

SUGGESTIONS
Beech branches with daffodils
Oak branches with roses
Maple or pine branches with chrysanthemums
Tree ivy with tulips

MEASUREMENTS
Shin—width of container plus depth and half as much again.
Soe—three-quarters of *shin*.
Hikae—three-quarters of *soe*.

17 The basic upright *moribana* style: hawthorn and iris in a pottery container

This is always an impressive arrangement. It has strength and vigour and, because of this, it is also rather dramatic. Its power derives from its overall upright appearance, which embodies the feeling of life and growth. It is certainly the arrangement I would recommend for any very special occasion.

The beginner might find it helpful, in attaining the right effect, to think of the three main stems in terms of what they represent: heaven, man and earth (here 'man' refers to mankind). In this arrangement man stands between heaven and earth, giving a concept of the whole universe, everything reaching outwards and upwards, vibrant with the life force. It is the direction taken by your *shin* line that will determine the position of the *kenzan* in the container. If it is to incline to the right, the *kenzan* will be placed in the left front of the container.

Shin is then fixed in the back of the *kenzan* centrally and slanted diagonally towards the right front so that its tip is at an angle of 10° from the imaginary vertical zero.

Soe comes next, in the right front of the *kenzan*, slanted diagonally towards the right front with its tip at an angle of 45° from the vertical zero.

Hikae follows, in the left front of the *kenzan* and slanted diagonally towards the left front with its tip at an angle of 75° from the vertical zero.

The angling of *soe* and *hikae* towards the front is very important. Neither of them should stick out starkly to the side. Inclining them forwards ensures the desired three-dimensional look.

When the three main stems are in position, the *jushi* are added. I might repeat that there is no measurement laid down for these but, however many you use, they will be of varying lengths and none will be longer than the main stem it supplements. They are placed in the central part of the *kenzan* at the base of the main stems, and they should be angled so that they lean out towards the viewer. Remember that everything must reach towards the sun, that is, you.

Bear in mind, too, that you must not be able to see any part of the *kenzan* from three feet in front of the finished arrangement. Leaves from the flowers, small stones or pebbles can be used to hide it. Do not just throw them in haphazardly. Place them carefully, so that they play a natural part in the arrangement and do not look like camouflage.

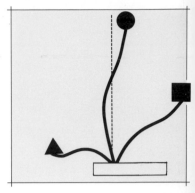

Fig. 8 The *risshin-kei* (basic upright style)

18 The basic slanting *moribana* style: japonica and Sonia roses

Should your arrangement call for the *kenzan* to be in the right front of the container then of course the positions of the second and third placements will be reversed: that is, with *shin* still in the back centre of the *kenzan* but this time inclining to the left, *soe* will go in the left front of the *kenzan* and *hikae* in the right front. They all retain their respective angles.

KEISHIN-KEI (BASIC SLANTING STYLE)

SUGGESTIONS
Pussy-willow with jonquils
Oak branches with tulips
Willow with small dahlias
Bare branches with chrysanthemums

MEASUREMENTS

Shin—width of container plus depth and half as much again.
Soe—three-quarters of *shin*.
Hikae—three-quarters of *soe*.

Because of the angle at which the *shin* is inserted, there is an overall slanting effect to this style of arrangement—as though the branches and flowers were bending before the wind. It is hardly surprising, therefore, that this is also known as the windswept style.

Thinking again of the main stems as heaven, man and earth, we get a rather different picture. This time man stands above heaven and earth—which might be taken to imply that the Japanese were foreseeing the future and anticipating space travel. It is more probable, however, that what they had in mind was philosophical rather than scientific: that the spirit of man transcends the heavens, and that heaven is not only above but also all around us wherever we might be. It is something to ponder.

If the sweep of the arrangement is to be to the left, place the *kenzan* in the right back or front of the container.

Since man is to rise above heaven, the positions of the stems in the previous arrangement are interchanged.

Shin is secured in the left front of the *kenzan* and slanted diagonally towards the left front with its tip at an angle of 45° from the vertical zero.

Soe goes in the back centre of the *kenzan*, slanted diagonally towards the left front with its tip at an angle of 10° from the vertical zero.

Hikae is placed in the right front of the *kenzan*, slanted diagonally towards the right front with its tip at an angle of 75° from the vertical zero.

The *jushi* are added in the centre and to the left of the *kenzan*, so that they follow the *shin* line. This does not mean that they have to be at the same angle as that line. They merely supplement it—and even if they are upright the overall slanting appearance will be maintained.

For an arrangement that sweeps to the right, the *kenzan* will be in the left back or front of the container, *shin* will be in the right front of it and *hikae* in the left front, retaining their respective angles. *Soe*, still at the back, will incline to the right front.

Be sure that the *kenzan* is concealed.

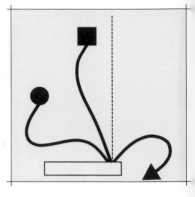

Fig. 9 The *keishin-kei* (basic slanting style)

RISSHIN-KEI NO. 1 OYO (VARIATION NO. 1)

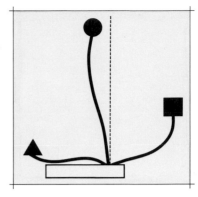

Fig. 10 *Risshin-kei* No. 1 *Oyo*

SUGGESTIONS
Whitebeam with daffodils
Weeping willow with iris
Magnolia branches with arum lilies
Bare branches with chrysanthemums

MEASUREMENTS
Shin—width of container plus depth and half as much again.
Soe—three-quarters of *shin*.
Hikae—three-quarters of *soe*.

Incidentally, *oyo* means 'style' in Japanese. This variation is also known as the 'open' style. Its object is to create an illusion of spaciousness, signifying, perhaps, the vastness of the universe.

The three main stems take the same relative positions they hold in the basic upright style, but with one significant difference, and that is the direction in which the *shin* line is slanted. Before, it followed the same direction as *soe*; now, these two lines must be kept as far apart as possible.

With the *kenzan* in the right front of the container, *Shin* is fixed in the left back of the *kenzan*, slanted diagonally towards the left with its tip at an angle of 10° from the vertical zero.

Soe goes in the right back of the *kenzan*, slanted diagonally towards the right back with its tip at an angle of 45° from the vertical zero.

Hikae goes in the left front of the *kenzan*, slanted diagonally towards the left front with its tip at an angle of 75° from the vertical zero.

It can be seen that *shin* and *soe* are virtually opposite each other but *soe* is slanted back to give further depth.

In order not to spoil the effect, very few *jushi* should be added in the centre of the *kenzan*. If they are kept fairly low they will help to accentuate the open look.

If the *kenzan* is required in the left front of the container, then *shin* will slant diagonally to the right rear, *soe* will go in the left front and *hikae* in the right front—all retaining their respective angles.

Do not forget to cover the *kenzan*.

19 *Moribana* variation No. 2: mahonia branches and pink carnations. *Right*, insertion of *shin, soe* and *hikae* and *left*, the finished arrangement

RISSHIN-KEI NO. 2 OYO
(VARIATION NO. 2)

SUGGESTIONS
Flowering currant, cherry- or apple-blossom
Sweet-chestnut branches with tulips
Oak branches with roses
Pine branches with chrysanthemums

MEASUREMENTS
Shin—width of container plus depth and half as much again.
Soe—three-quarters of *shin*.
Hikae—three-quarters of *soe*.

Another name for this arrangement is 'main branch interchange'. In it, the *shin* line retains the position it holds in the basic upright style but the *soe* and *hikae* lines change places. This means that heaven and earth stand above man, and it might be thought to represent the humility of man before the wonders of heaven and earth.

With the *kenzan* in the left-hand side of the container, *shin* is placed in the back centre and slanted diagonally towards the right front with its tip at an angle of 10° from the vertical zero.

Soe is placed in the right front of the *kenzan*, slanted diagonally towards the front with its tip at an angle of 75° from the vertical zero.

Hikae is placed in the left front of the *kenzan*, slanted diagonally towards the left front with its tip at an angle of 45° from the vertical zero.

By this simple interchange of the main branches a completely different look is given to the *risshin-kei*.

Jushi are added in the centre of the *kenzan*, which must, of course, be concealed.

With the *kenzan* in the right-hand side of the container, the positions of *soe* and *hikae* will be reversed. *Soe* will go in the left front of the *kenzan* and *hikae* in the right front, retaining their respective angles.

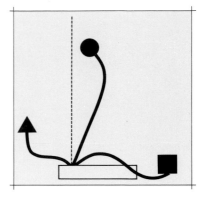

Fig. 11 *Risshin-kei* No. 2 *Oyo*

KEISHIN-KEI NO. 3 OYO (VARIATION NO. 3)

SUGGESTIONS
Chestnut branches with iris
Tulips only, or roses
Berberis with roses
Cedar branches with chrysanthemums

MEASUREMENTS
Shin—width of container plus depth and half as much again.
Soe—three-quarters of *shin*.
Hikae—three-quarters of *soe*.

Also known as the fan-shape arrangement, this variation is eminently suited to all kinds of flowers and can, in fact, be done with flowers alone. A fan-shape of tulips, roses or chrysanthemums will look even more effective in a western-style room than it does in a Japanese room. For this form is more akin to western flower arrangement, when only flowers are used, than any other. I like to use a combination of branches and flowers to illustrate this type of arrangement but that need not discourage you from experimenting. No matter what you use, the method of going about it is always the same.

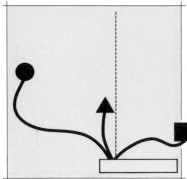

Fig. 12 *Keishin-kei* No. 3 *Oyo*

20 *Moribana* variation No. 3:
aspidistra leaves and a yellow lily

With the *kenzan* to the left of the container, *shin* is fixed in the back left of the *kenzan*, slanting diagonally towards the left with its tip at an angle of 45° from the vertical zero.

Soe goes in the right back of the *kenzan*, slanting diagonally towards the right with its tip at an angle of 75° from the vertical zero.

Hikae goes in the centre front of the *kenzan*, slanting diagonally towards the front with its tip at an angle of 10° from the vertical zero. It is the opening out of *shin* and *soe* in opposite directions, with *hikae* facing the front, that gives the fan-like appearance.

Jushi are added in the centre of the *kenzan* — and the *kenzan* must be hidden.

With the *kenzan* in the right-hand side of the container, *shin*, in the back right of the *kenzan*, inclines to the right, *soe* goes in the left back and inclines to the left, and *hikae* goes in the centre front and inclines to the front. The respective angles remain the same.

RISSHIN-KEI NO. 4 OYO (VARIATION NO. 4)

SUGGESTIONS
Weeping willow with iris
Snapdragons with leaves
Beech branches with arum lilies
Pine branches with roses

MEASUREMENTS
Shin — width of container plus depth and half as much again.
Hikae — one-third of *shin*.

I have not forgotten to include a measurement. The omission of *soe* is deliberate and, in fact, this variation is sometimes called 'the arrangement of omission'. Because it is man who is not represented, it is also known as 'the arrangement of humility'. But it is most frequently referred to as 'the one-and-one arrangement'.

No matter what you choose to call it, with only *shin* and *hikae* appearing this is always a rather narrow arrangement. It is also very striking and somewhat dramatic. All teachers are permitted a favourite, and this one is mine. (It is illustrated on p. 41.)

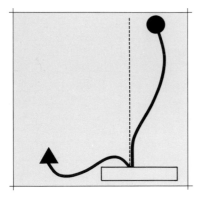

Fig. 13 *Risshin-kei* No. 4 *Oyo*

With the *kenzan* placed to the left of the container, *shin* is fixed in the back of the *kenzan* and slanted diagonally towards the right with its tip at an angle of 10° from the vertical zero.

Hikae goes in the front of the *kenzan*, slanted diagonally towards the left front with its tip at an angle of 75° from the vertical zero.

The use of only two main branches emphasizes the stark simplicity that is the basis of all Japanese arrangements.

Jushi are added in the centre of the *kenzan*—which will be artfully hidden—and here again, the fewer the better.

If you want the *kenzan* in the right of the container, *shin* will slant diagonally towards the left and *hikae* towards the right front, at their respective angles.

RISSHIN-KEI NO. 5 OYO
(VARIATION NO. 5)

SUGGESTIONS
Reeds with iris
Hawthorn branches with daffodils
Beech branches with roses
Rhododendron branches with chrysanthemums

MEASUREMENTS
Shin—width of container plus depth and half as much again.
Soe—three-quarters of *shin*.
Hikae—three-quarters of *soe*.

Thus far the variations have consisted of simple alterations to the positioning of the main stems in the *kenzan*, but in this—the divided *kenzan* arrangement—we depart from what has become the norm by using a second *kenzan*.

Since two *kenzan* are to be used, it will be obvious that this is a fairly large arrangement which will call for a correspondingly large container. It is also an arrangement which has in itself a good deal of variety, depending upon which stems are placed in which *kenzan*. Basically, the *kenzan* are diagonally opposite each other in the container, one holding the *shin* and *soe* lines, the other holding *hikae*. This means that if *shin* and *soe* are in the

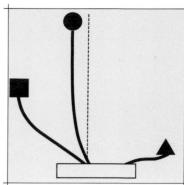

Fig. 14 *Risshin-kei* No. 5 *Oyo*, with two *kenzan*

21 Moribana Variation No. 5: white chrysanthemum, mahonia, driftwood

left front of the container then *hikae* must be in the right rear; and if they are in the right front then *hikae* must be in the left rear. Alternatively, if *hikae* is in either of the front positions then *shin* and *soe* must be in the diagonally opposite rear position.

If the two taller branches are to the front of your arrangement, the perspective you get is that of looking down an avenue of trees, where those nearest you appear huge and those in the distance seem quite small. With the larger ones at the rear it might be compared with a view of mountainous country, where everything in the foreground is dwarfed by the towering background.

For the purpose of practice, place one *kenzan* in the front left of the container and the other in the right rear.

FRONT KENZAN
Shin is placed in the back centre of the *kenzan*, slanting diagonally towards the left with its tip at an angle of 10° from the vertical zero.

Soe is placed in the front of the *kenzan*, slanting diagonally towards the left with its tip at an angle of 45° from the vertical zero.

REAR KENZAN

Hikae is placed in the back centre of the *kenzan*, slanting diagonally towards the right with its tip at an angle of 75° from the vertical zero—the vertical zero, in this case, being calculated from the point where *hikae* is fixed in the *kenzan*.

Jushi are added in the centre of each *kenzan*. But this does not complete the arrangement. If it is left like this it is going to look like two separate arrangements in one container. So not only do both *kenzan* have to be concealed but they must also be linked. This can be done with driftwood or small stones, but it must be done subtly. One or two straight lines of stones from one *kenzan* to the other will destroy all illusion. Place the stones carefully in curved or irregular lines, to look as if the water has been washing over them; and have some in the front of the container and some at the back. Driftwood, too, must be carefully placed in order to look as careless as nature intended. These fine finishing touches are worth every bit of extra time and trouble, for this arrangement is always reminiscent of an outdoor scene and can be breathtaking if done properly.

If *hikae* is in the front left *kenzan* and *shin* and *soe* are in the right rear one, then *hikae* will incline towards the left and the other two towards the right, all retaining their respective angles.

A variation of the divided *kenzan* can be effected by having *shin* and *hikae* in one *kenzan* and *soe* in the other. The direction taken by the placements would still be governed by the position of *shin* and each would incline at its customary angle.

HORIZONTAL STYLE (VARIATION NO. 6)

SUGGESTIONS
Peony leaves with rhododendron flowers
Beech branches with daffodils
Oak branches with tiger-lilies
Pine branches with chrysanthemums

MEASUREMENTS
Shin—to depend on the size and shape of the table.
Soe—three-quarters of *shin*.
Hikae—three-quarters of *soe*.

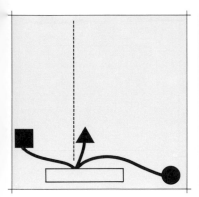

Fig. 15 *Keishin-kei* No. 6 *Oyo*, the horizontal style. The *hikae* looks more upright than it is because it inclines to the rear

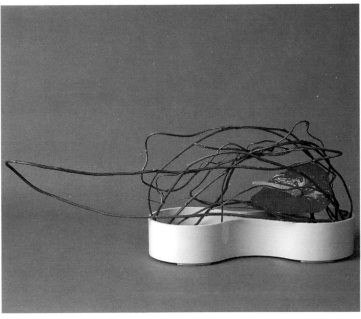

22 Horizontal *moribana* style, variation No. 6: Japanese vine and anthurium in a container designed by Hiroshi Teshigahara

Unlike the foregoing variations, which are all for frontal viewing only, the horizontal style is designed as a centrepiece for the dining-table and will therefore be seen from all sides. It is, of necessity, a low arrangement, for although you will want it to be admired it must not be obtrusive. Nothing could be more irritating to guests than to have a branch or flower tip disturbing their line of vision and causing them to look slightly cross-eyed at their opposite number at table.

The overall size of the arrangement is not this time determined by the size of the container but by the size and shape of the dining-table. It is a decision that must depend solely on your own judgement. Quite obviously, a large arrangement would be impractical on a small table and a small arrangement would look completely lost on a massive table.

With the *kenzan* in the left-hand side of the container, fix *shin* in the right front of the *kenzan* and slant it diagonally towards the right front so that it is almost horizontal, with its tip at an angle of about 85° from the vertical zero.

Soe goes in the left front of the *kenzan*, slanted diagonally towards the left front with its tip at an angle of between 60° and 70° from the vertical zero.

Hikae goes in the back centre of the *kenzan*, slanted directly to the rear with its tip at an angle of 75° from the vertical zero.

23 A *morimono* arrangement: sharon fruit (a variety of persimmon), green grapes and flowering currant branches in a Japanese lacquered box (*see also* p. 92)

Care must be taken in placing *shin* to ensure that it clears the rim of the container. This arrangement, as much as any other, must have the appearance of life and growth. A tired-looking branch resting on the rim of the container can be ruinous.

Jushi can be used here almost with abandon. They are added in the centre of the *kenzan* and should be angled so that they face out in all directions between the main stems. But they must, of course, be kept very low.

Particular attention needs to be paid to the covering of the *kenzan* so that it cannot be seen from above or from any side.

When the weather is warm it is a nice idea to have plenty of water visible in the container. The effect is cooling and refreshing.

With the *kenzan* in the right-hand side of the container, *shin* will go in the left front of the *kenzan* and slant towards the left front, *soe* will go in the right front and slant towards the right front, and *hikae* will still go directly towards the rear—all at the same respective angles.

MORIMONO (VARIATION NO. 7)

SUGGESTIONS
Pineapple, lemons and daffodils
Green peppers, peony leaves and rosebuds
Grapes with arum lilies
Apples with chrysanthemums

To attempt to give measurements for the *morimono* style would only be confusing, for here we have the combination of fruit or vegetables with flowers. The emphasis, therefore, is on colour and shape. And it is in this arrangement that you are thrown at once on to your own inventiveness and resourcefulness.

The variety of material is endless and the best advice is to experiment boldly without worrying too much about rules and regulations.

Nevertheless, the basic principles and the basic arrangements already attempted can still serve as a useful guide. For though you may not find, say, one apple that is three-quarters the size of another apple and a flower that is three-quarters the size of that, you can think of these things as *shin, soe* and *hikae* and position them so that

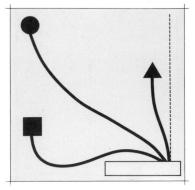

Fig. 16 *Morimono* (variation No. 7)

they give the triangular effect given by the three main stems in the more conventional arrangements.

An arrangement following the lines of the now familiar ones can be effected with fruit and flowers, and you can experiment here, where the three main stems will approximate to their usual 10°, 45° and 75° angles—even though one 'stem' is a piece of fruit. These can be done in shallow bowls and dishes, on platters, or simply on large leaves such as palm or banana leaves. The aim is to employ the various shapes, textures and colours so that they make a harmonious whole; and if you have been practising the other arrangements you will have a very good idea of what constitutes a pleasing picture. There are other forms of *morimono* which can be done in or out of water, with or without a *kenzan*, and even without a container.

A floating arrangement can be made by filling a plate with water and placing a branch in it so that it lies across it diagonally. The tip of the branch should curve over the edge of the plate, and *jushi* are floated on the water close to the stem of the branch.

The *shikibana* arrangement dispenses with the container entirely. Here a branch is placed directly on the table and flowers are added artistically on top of it. This is, of course, only a temporary table decoration and it cannot be expected to last very long. An example is shown in Plate 33 on p. 89.

All *morimono* arrangements make excellent table decorations.

COMBINATION ARRANGEMENT (VARIATION NO. 8)

SUGGESTIONS
Beech branches with roses
Azalea branches with gladioli
Rhododendron branches with carnations
Driftwood with chrysanthemums

MEASUREMENTS
Shin—width of container plus depth and half as much again.
Soe—three-quarters of *shin*.
Hikae—three-quarters of *soe*.

24 A combination arrangement
with skimmia, young shoots of
euonymus, hellebore and
anemones in two pottery
containers

If you have been making progress with the *risshin-kei* and *keishin-kei* styles, this variation will be welcomed as an opportunity to combine the two in one arrangement.

Since two containers are used, a certain amount of ingenuity is needed to ensure that there is a fusion between them. The viewer must be less conscious of two styles in two containers than of the overall picture of a single harmonious arrangement. This is not to say that the containers must be identical in shape, or even in colour. They can be quite different from each other just as long as they are not wildly contrasting. If you happen to possess matching containers, of course, you have no problem; otherwise, the maxim is harmony of colour, shape and texture between the two containers.

But the matter of containers does not end here. It is clear that if they are to combine in one arrangement they must be quite close to each other—and yet the line of one style must not interfere with or obscure the line of the other. As both containers will be shallow—for we are still dealing with the *moribana* form—the only way to preserve the individual lines of the two styles is to have them in different planes. One container must therefore be on a higher level than the other, and most appropriate is the type which has small pedestal legs. It is an extremely popular type, easily obtainable, manufactured in varying shapes, colours and sizes, and is particularly well suited to Japanese arrangements. Failing this, one container might stand on a piece of driftwood or a small dais. Whatever you use, however, must be in keeping with the arrangement: books will not do.

Once you have decided on containers—let us say an ordinary flat one and one with pedestal legs—the flat one will be placed in front of and to the left or right of the pedestal, depending on the direction of the arrangement. If it is to sweep to the right, the flat container will be to the right front of the pedestal. To maintain their clarity of line, both styles will incline towards the same direction and the tallest—the *risshin-kei*—will be on the higher level.

The two styles follow their customary pattern and I need only briefly remind you of them here.

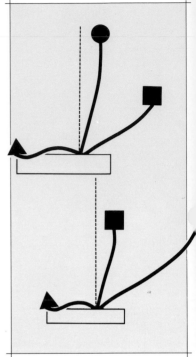

Fig. 17 The combination arrangement (variation No. 8)

REAR CONTAINER: RISSHIN-KEI
Kenzan—right front of container.
Shin—back centre of *kenzan*, slanted diagonally towards right front with tip at an angle of 10° from vertical zero.

Soe—right front of *kenzan*, slanted diagonally towards right front with its tip at an angle of 45° from the vertical zero.
Hikae—left front of *kenzan*, slanted diagonally towards left front with its tip at an angle of 75° from the vertical zero.

FRONT CONTAINER: KEISHIN-KEI
Kenzan—right front of container.
Shin—right front of *kenzan*, slanted diagonally towards right front with its tip at an angle of 45° from the vertical zero.
Soe—back centre of *kenzan*, slanted diagonally towards right front with its tip at an angle of 10° from the vertical zero.
Hikae—left front of *kenzan*, slanted diagonally towards left front with its tip at an angle of 75° from the vertical zero.
Jushi are added to each style in the centre of the *kenzan*.

If the arrangement is to sweep to the left, the flat container will be to the left of the pedestal and the placements in each style will be reversed.

The usual care will, of course, be taken to ensure that the *kenzan* in each container is completely hidden.

This style of the combination arrangement, using the basic upright and the basic slanting, is the simplest. But by the time you are ready to start practising the arrangement you should have more or less mastered the basic styles and may be feeling rather adventurous. Nevertheless, it is a good plan to try first with the two basics. Thereafter you can let your eye decide whether to use them or any of their variations in combination—allowing your material to suggest how best it might be employed.

Perhaps it is fitting that this section on *moribana* arrangements, which began with individual descriptions of the basic upright and basic slanting styles, should end with an arrangement in which these two main styles are combined. But it cannot really be called an end: it should actually be considered a beginning, for here are the rudiments of all that you will do in the future.

All the arrangements given here can be practised any number of times without the exercise becoming boring or seeming repetitive, for even with the same material you will not get exactly the same result twice. And constant practice will give you the deftness and confidence that so greatly encourage creative self-expression.

CHAPTER V

BASIC NAGEIRE ARRANGEMENTS

Literally translated, *nageire* means 'thrown in'. But do not let that mislead you. Its wider meaning is 'natural' or 'casual-looking', which is what a finished arrangement should be. Achieving an artless appearance is, however, an art in itself.

The firm fixing of material in the container is of no less importance in *nageire* arrangements than it is in *moribana*. It will be obvious, though, that the *kenzan* cannot be used in tall, upright containers—and it is this that makes *nageire* the more difficult style of the two. Such methods of securing material as are used in some western flower arrangements, should you know them, are best forgotten. Chicken-wire, plasticine and chewing-gum are absolutely taboo. Aesthetic reasons apart, they would not give adequate support for the type of material you would be working with. The only accepted techniques of control are those I am about to explain. You will need to master them before you begin a *nageire* arrangement.

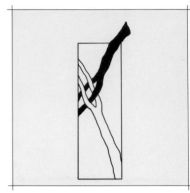

Fig. 18 The vertical fixture

VERTICAL FIXTURE

This is the simplest and possibly the most widely used control because it is effective in any upright container, regardless of shape. It is made by cutting a fairly substantial branch to a little less than the height of the container and then splitting it centrally at one end to an extent of about three inches (8 cm). Stand it in the container with the split end uppermost and touching the wall of the container. The next step is to split the stem of the branch you wish to secure, also for about three inches, and insert it so that the forked ends of the branches interlock. With the ends of the arrangement branch and the fixture resting against the wall of the container you can be sure of maximum security. All the branches in your arrangement can be thus controlled by the vertical fixture.

If the material you are using is particularly slender, make its security doubly sure by tying the branches together with florist's wire or twine at the intersection.

25 The basic upright *nageire* style: cherry-blossom and mahonia

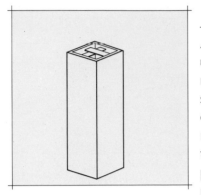

Fig. 19 The cross-bar fixture

CROSS-BAR FIXTURE

Also simple in its construction, the cross-bar should be used only in containers that are cylindrical in shape. To make it you will need two small but sturdy twigs, cut to a size that will enable them to be wedged firmly in the neck of the container about half an inch (1 cm) down from the rim. When you have tried them for size, tie the twigs together in the form of a cross and replace them in position. If the twigs fit really snugly, tying may not be necessary.

Branches can then be inserted at their various angles so that the ends of the stems rest against the wall of the container while the cross-bar takes their weight. If you have cut your branches correctly, their slanting ends will ensure that their water supply is not cut off if they should touch the wall of the container.

Depending on the nature of your material, branches can be tied to the actual fixture. You will be able to judge the necessity for yourself.

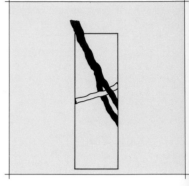

Fig. 20 The single-bar fixture

SINGLE-BAR FIXTURE

The single-bar is particularly effective in securing a branch that is not well proportioned. Its application is similar to that of the cross-bar, in that you will require a strong twig of a length that will enable it to be wedged within the container. This time, however, it will be necessary to split the stem of the branch you are going to use to an extent of about three inches (8 cm). The twig is then placed in the fork of the split stem and tied in position with wire or twine.

It only remains, when putting the branch in the container, to ensure that the ends of the twig are firmly wedged inside the container.

FIXTURE FOR JARS

Containers of the jar type need something rather different in the way of a fixture. Their width makes it impractical to use either the single-bar or the cross-bar, and even the vertical fixture might not be entirely reliable. So for these containers you will need two branches, one to stand in the container and measuring just a little less than its height, the other to wedge across it just below its opening.

Fig. 21 The fixture for jars

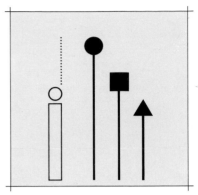

Fig. 22 Standard *nageire* measurements. The stem lengths shown here do not include an allowance to go inside the container

These branches are tied together at the point where they cross and your arrangement branch is tied to them at the desired angle. When placing this fixture in the container it is important to see that the upright branch is standing firmly on the base of the container, while the ends of the cross-piece are firm against the inside walls.

The current method of teaching basic arrangements is to alternate *moribana* and *nageire*, but I feel that when you actually attempt *nageire* arrangements you will appreciate what it means to be thoroughly practised in *moribana*. At first glance you might well wonder what is so difficult about it—after all, the basic *nageire* styles are exactly the same as those in the *moribana* form. Why, then, should they be harder to accomplish? The answer lies in the very nature of *nageire*—an apparently casual arrangement of material in tall containers.

To begin with, a tall container offers only a very limited space in which to manoeuvre material. It is an advantage, therefore, to be familiar with the handling of branches and the parts they play in each style.

There is also the matter of securing material in the container. The fixtures already mentioned may seem daunting to the beginner. They are soon mastered with practice, but they are certainly not as easy to work with as the *kenzan*. Again, the experience gained in the handling of material in *moribana* arrangements will serve you in good stead here.

The little extra patience that *nageire* requires is more than compensated for by results. Arrangements in tall, slender containers can be superlatively graceful and beautiful, and they look perfect in western surroundings. They are more constricted than *moribana* styles and do not have the same scenic quality, but they do maintain the tendency to follow nature and present the material as living and growing. For this reason the three-dimensional look is sought as much as ever. And there must be harmony between the container and the material.

It is important to remember that the measurements for *nageire* arrangements indicate the length of branch to be seen above the rim of the container. Allowance must always be made for the extra length which will be inside the container—enough at least to ensure that the branch can be firmly fixed and also receive a supply of water.

The type of fixture used will depend on the shape of the container and the weight of the material—at first, no doubt, a matter of trial and error. But the choice of material is endless, and the suggestions which preface the styles are, as I have said previously, only guides.

RISSHIN-KEI (BASIC UPRIGHT STYLE)

SUGGESTIONS
Beech branches with alstroemeria
Oak branches with roses
Rhododendron branches with carnations
Bare branches with chrysanthemums

MEASUREMENTS
Shin—depth of container plus width and half as much again above rim of container.
Soe—three-quarters of *shin* above rim of container.
Hikae—three-quarters of *soe* above rim of container.

Using the cross-bar fixture, place it in the container so that it crosses diagonally as you face it, about half an inch down from the rim. You will then use whichever segment is appropriate to the direction of your arrangement.

Shin is inserted so that it rests firmly against the cross-bar, slanted diagonally towards the right front with its tip at an angle of 10° from the vertical zero.

Soe follows in the same segment, slanted diagonally towards the right front with its tip at an angle of 45° from the vertical zero.

Hikae also goes in the same segment, slanted diagonally towards the left front with its tip at an angle of 75° from the vertical zero.

Alternatively, if *shin* and *soe* incline towards the left front the *hikae* will incline towards the right front, each retaining its own angle.

Jushi are added in the same segment as the main stems.

If the vertical fixture is used, the base of the *shin* stem will be split and interlocked with the fixture. *Soe* will receive the same treatment but need not necessarily be attached to the fixture. If it is more convenient, it can be wedged on to the lower part of the *shin* branch itself. *Hikae*, being the shortest piece, does not have to be split at all. Just bending and twisting the lower part of the stem will be sufficient to keep it in place.

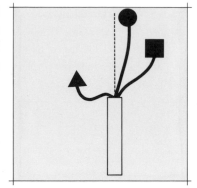

Fig. 23 The *risshin-kei* (basic upright style)

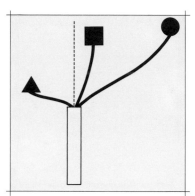

Fig. 24 The *keishin-kei* (basic slanting style)

26 The basic slanting *nageire* style: camellia and blackthorn

There is more laxity here than in the *moribana* style and, though it is desirable for the material to have the appearance of flowing from the container, it is permissible for branches to rest on its rim.

KEISHIN-KEI (BASIC SLANTING STYLE)

SUGGESTIONS
Camellia branches with freesia
Broom with carnations
Beech branches with spray chrysanthemums
Pine branches with roses

MEASUREMENTS
Shin – depth of container plus width and half as much again above rim of container.
Soe – three-quarters of *shin* above rim of container.
Hikae – three-quarters of *soe* above rim of container.

With whichever fixture you use, *shin* is inserted to the right front of the container, slanted diagonally towards the right front with its tip at an angle of 45° from the vertical zero.

Soe, to the rear centre of the fixture, is slanted diagonally towards the right front with its tip at an angle of 10° from the vertical zero.

Hikae, to the left front of the fixture, is slanted diagonally towards the left front with its tip at an angle of 75° from the vertical zero.

Should you want *shin* and *soe* slanting towards the left front, *hikae* will slant towards the right front, all retaining their respective angles.

Jushi are added in the centre and at the bases of the main stems.

RISSHIN-KEI NO. 1 OYO (VARIATION NO. 1)

SUGGESTIONS
Oak branches with jonquils
Apple-blossom with snapdragons
Willow branches with iris
Bare branches with chrysanthemums

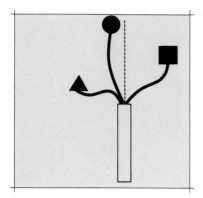

Fig. 25 *Risshin-kei* No. 1 *Oyo*

27 *Nageire* variation No. 1: rhododendron branches with a yellow lily. *Right*, insertion of *shin*, *soe* and *hikae* and *left*, the finished arrangement

MEASUREMENTS

Shin – depth of container plus width and half as much again above rim of container.

Soe – three-quarters of *shin* above rim of container.

Hikae – three-quarters of *soe* above rim of container.

This, you may recall, is the 'open' style, which has as much space as possible between *shin* and *soe*.

Shin is secured in the fixture so that it slants diagonally towards the left with its tip at an angle of 10° from the vertical zero.

Soe is inserted so that it slants diagonally towards the right rear with its tip at an angle of 45° from the vertical zero. This gives the arrangement as much depth as possible.

Hikae goes in so that it slants diagonally towards the left front with its tip at an angle of 75° from the vertical zero.

If *shin* slants towards the right rear, *soe* will slant towards the left front and *hikae* towards the right front, keeping their respective angles.

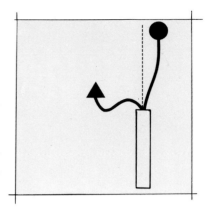

Fig. 26 *Risshin-kei* No. 4 *Oyo*

Jushi are added sparingly and kept low in order to maintain the open look.

In this arrangement *soe* and *hikae* are interchangeable. There is no rule about it and you can be guided only by your material and your own judgement as to how it might best be displayed.

Having stressed the difficulty of creating *nageire* arrangements, it may seem that I have given them rather cursory treatment here. The point is, however, that their problems are related to practice, not theory. All the *nageire* style variations are identical to those of *moribana*, even to the numbering of the variations. Consequently I have chosen to illustrate only No. 4, and No. 8 which is a combination *moribana* and *nageire* arrangement. If you have been practising the *moribana* styles you are more than half-way to success. For the rest, I do not think that any amount of writing on my part can take the place of constant practice in helping you to become accustomed to using the various fixtures and to working within the confines of a narrow-necked container.

RISSHIN-KEI NO. 4 OYO (VARIATION NO. 1)

SUGGESTIONS
Willow branches with tulips
Broom with foliage or iris
Oak branches with snapdragons
Pine branches with chrysanthemums

MEASUREMENTS
Shin — depth of container plus width and half as much again above rim of container.
Hikae — one-third of *shin* above rim of container.

In this, the arrangement of omission, it may well be that a single forked twig wedged between the walls of the container will be sufficient to secure the two main branches. But you will, of course, choose the type of fixture most suited to the material with which you are working.

Shin is inserted so that it slants diagonally towards the right with its tip at an angle of 10° from the vertical zero.

Hikae is slanted diagonally towards the left front with its tip at an angle of 75° from the vertical zero.

28 *Nageire* variation No. 4: willow tortuoso painted black, dried wood and a yellow rose

If *shin* slants towards the left, *hikae* will slant towards the right front, at the same respective angles.

Jushi are added in the centre and should be kept to a minimum.

COMBINATION ARRANGEMENT (VARIATION NO. 8)

SUGGESTIONS
Viburnum with anthurium
Hornbeam with roses
Beech branches with chrysanthemums
Yew branches with dahlias

MEASUREMENTS
Shin—depth of container plus width and half as much again (above rim of container for *nageire*).
Soe—three-quarters of *shin* (above rim of container for *nageire*).
Hikae—three-quarters of *soe* (above rim of container for *nageire*).

This can well be looked on as the culmination of all you have learned, for it combines not only the two basic styles but also the two basic forms in one arrangement. The effectiveness of the two styles together will have been seen in the *moribana* version of this arrangement. Now the effect is heightened by the introduction of *nageire*.

Although the containers used must, of necessity, be entirely different from each other in shape—one low, the other tall—there must nevertheless be harmony between them regarding colour and texture. The aim is one complete picture, not two separate arrangements standing next to one another.

Again, clarity of line is of the utmost importance. The branches of one style should never be in contact with or cut across the branches of the other. For this reason the tall style—*risshin-kei*—will be in the tall *nageire* container.

The position of the *moribana* container is always in front of and to the left or right of the *nageire*, depending on the sweep of the arrangement.

You may or may not be quite familiar with the positions of the placements in both the styles by now; but to save you looking them up, it is worth repeating them here.

29 The combination *moribana* and *nageire* arrangement: mahonia and anthuriums with a stripped branch of pine

NAGEIRE CONTAINER (REAR): RISSHIN-KEI
Appropriate fixture.
Shin—slanted diagonally towards left front with its tip at an angle of 10° from the vertical zero.
Soe—slanted diagonally towards left front with its tip at an angle of 45° from the vertical zero.
Hikae—slanted diagonally towards right front with its tip at an angle of 75° from the vertical zero.

MORIBANA CONTAINER (FRONT): KEISHIN-KEI
Kenzan—left front of container.
Shin—right front of *kenzan*, slanted diagonally towards right front with its tip at an angle of 45° from the vertical zero.
Soe—back centre of *kenzan*, slanted diagonally towards right front with its tip at an angle of 10° from the vertical zero.
Hikae—left front of *kenzan*, slanted diagonally towards left front with its tip at an angle of 75° from the vertical zero.

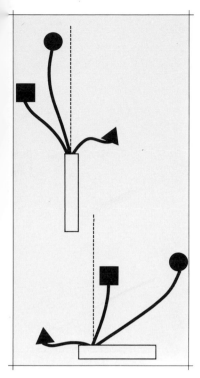

Fig. 27 The combination *moribana* and *nageire* arrangement

If the *moribana* container is to the left front of the *nageire*, the direction in which the main stems slant will be reversed in each style. They will, of course, retain their respective angles.

Jushi are added in the centre of each style at the base of the main stems. And the *kenzan* in the *moribana* container must be concealed.

As I pointed out in the *moribana* combination arrangement, you are by no means bound to combine only the basic arrangements. Any of the *moribana* and *nageire* variations may be combined in this arrangement—provided they make a harmonious whole.

If the words 'constant practice' crop up frequently in these pages it is not by chance. Only practice can lead to proficiency. Remember that the aim of the Sogetsu School is to encourage individuality and the freedom of self-expression, and that there is no need to become too preoccupied with angles and measurements. By sticking to them as closely as possible in the early stages you can be sure of pleasing and even exciting results. Later, when you have the feel of your material and your imagination will not want to be bound, you can alternate them, deviate from them or even abandon them completely. Rulers, set-squares and protractors are not part of a flower arranger's equipment. At best, the angles and measurements need only be an approximation—with more laxity permitted the beginner in *nageire* than in *moribana* styles.

You have, then, within these three chapters of fundamentals, principles and basic arrangements, the groundwork for all you might wish to do in the field of Japanese flower arrangement.

CHAPTER VI

ADVANCED ARRANGEMENTS

In this chapter I am including free-style, abstract and avant-garde styles. While I will say something about them all, I will not provide a section on each, but rather concentrate more specifically on different kinds of materials, unusual containers, free-standing and no-container arrangements. The style you use is your choice. As I have said before, I am not going to embrace the latest style for its own sake. It seems to me to be much more important to learn to communicate your own thoughts and feelings through the medium of ikebana than to set out deliberately to shock or startle your family and friends.

That ikebana should change with the times is not surprising, but that the change should be as dramatic as it has been in the advanced styles is noteworthy. Sofu Teshigahara started something of a revolution nearly fifty years ago when he broke with the rigid formalities of the classic styles. But his ideas were gradually absorbed into the mainstream until they became what is today identified as the traditional in ikebana.

The newer styles have in common a basic element of design, the creation of a dramatic effect and a challenge to the arranger's creative ability. Gone is the old adherence to the traditional symbolism of *shin* (heaven), *soe* (earth) and *hikae* (man). However, the basic balance of opposites in the use of light and heavyweight material and contrasting colours is still important. And although the main placements are not in themselves representational, your overall arrangement can symbolize anything you wish. There may be occasions when a modern arrangement may look suspiciously like one of the now traditional styles from which it sprang. Do not let that worry you: it is not a fault.

The only serious mistake you can make is to attempt these arrangements before you are really ready for them. Remember that it took the Japanese centuries to bring ikebana to what it is today. I am not suggesting that it will take you an unconscionably long time, but you must be sure that you are sufficiently familiar with the basic styles before embarking on this new venture.

30 A swift-sailing boat: an abstract arrangement of Japanese reeds and dried elder branch with two boat-shaped containers (*see p. 94*)

Sofu Teshigahara has stated quite bluntly that the contemporary styles are for advanced students only. He did not like beginners to concern themselves with them or attempt to do them. And, of course, his reasoning was sound. An engineer cannot build a bridge without applying the basic principles of bridge-building; an architect cannot plan a building without applying the basic principles of architecture. The bridge might be unique, the building like none that has gone before it, but without a thorough knowledge of basic principles neither the engineer nor the architect could be sure that his creation would work.

So it is with flower arrangement. Freedom from rules does not mean wild abandon. Every arrangement, no matter how modern, still requires thought, care and a sense of purpose. And even if its meaning is obscure it should at least be pleasing to the eye.

Even fairly advanced students, I have found, are often inclined to lose their heads when first trying the new styles. Many of them feel compelled to cram as much material as they can into a container, with a grand disregard for everything they have been taught. But this hysteria soon wears off when they find that their 'creation' is no more than a hodge-podge of shrubbery, lacking in form and direction and without a vestige of visual appeal. It is then that their knowledge of the basic principles comes to the rescue and they rediscover the importance of line, the value of proportion and the need for care.

Contemporary styles fall into three distinct categories: modern free-style, abstract and avant-garde. Both the modern free-style and the abstract are referred to by the Japanese as *zokei*, which means 'changing of form' and relates to the bending of material from one shape to another.

MODERN FREE-STYLE

One of the first ideals to crumble before the onslaught of the vigorous new arrangers has been the sublimation of self to the material. The *moribana* style, itself a breakaway from hide-bound tradition, while presenting a freer way of arranging flowers, nevertheless requires that material is used in as natural a form as possible and that the nature of the material should dictate the form of the arrangement.

31 A free-style arrangement with orange lilies and peony leaves in three bamboo baskets (see p. 93)

These are not narrow restrictions, but they are restrictions just the same—and ones that the modern free-style sweeps lustily aside.

Here it is the arranger's unbridled imagination that counts, and all else is subjugated to it. The natural look is immaterial. Pattern rather than scenic effect is striven for and, where convenient, nature can be forgotten. Branches or flowers may hang downwards over the rim of the container, leaves may lie horizontally; anything pliable may be bent into unusual and outlandish curves. In short, anything goes. I suppose the line might be drawn at putting flowers in upside down, although I would not swear that this has not actually been done.

Main placements have no significance in the scheme of things other than to outline the height and width of the arrangement and to form part of the ultimate pattern. Their relationship to each other is purely fortuitous and contains no symbolic inference other than what the arranger chooses to give it.

Any material can be used—in or out of season, as simple or as exotic as you please. The only consideration is whether or not it will fit into the pattern you have in mind.

All this negation of old concepts does not mean that a free-style arrangement must break the rules in every possible way. More often than not, much of the material will appear in quite a natural fashion with just one or two placements flouting nature in order to give a particular effect. The final aim, remember, is a strikingly dramatic and, above all, attractive picture.

There can be no measurement strictures for arrangements which follow no set form, but a sense of balance is none the less an integral part of visual appeal. It is the arranger in whom a knowledge of the basic principles has been instilled, who has acquired an eye for visual balance, who is most unlikely to err in this respect. And it is a good enough reason to be thoroughly practised in the basic arrangements before attempting modern free-style. A lucky fluke might bring the beginner to a pleasing result—but it is a rare chance.

The touch of genius cannot be taught and neither, strictly speaking, can the modern free-style. It must evolve for the beginner, as it did in historical fact, from the basic *moribana* and *nageire* arrangements. When my own students are ready to tackle it, I simply hand them some

32 Two beautiful glass containers hold senecio branches and dahlias (see p. 94)

material and tell them to get on with it. The most I can do thereafter is to offer constructive criticism.

ABSTRACT

The differences between abstract and free-style arrangements are not so great as to be immediately obvious to the uninitiated. A clue is to be found, however, in the fact that the abstract style is also known as the 'non-realistic' – which means that it does not relate to anything that grows. This is going further than occasionally forgetting nature in order to gain an effect. It discounts nature from the very outset and the natural growth of the material has no bearing at all on its use.

Geometric design is the inspiration for abstract arrangements—strong, well-defined lines and sharp, clear-cut angles which call mainly for the use of quite straight material. The shape of a container might well spark off the basic idea for a complementary or contrasting design. The three-dimensional look is definitely out, for the abstract benefits greatly in dramatic effect from its sometimes flat and contrived appearance. And though the arranger might intend to convey some sort of message, none of the material has a special designation, and traditional Japanese symbolism is in no way involved. The driving force need, in fact, be no greater than the desire to make an unusual and striking arrangement.

AVANT-GARDE

Contemplating the growth of ikebana and the changes it has undergone, from its very beginnings to the modern free and abstract styles, might prompt the reader to ask what comes next. The startling answer is the avant-garde. Not only does this style divorce itself from every recognized concept of Japanese flower arrangement, it also, in the process, dispenses with flowers entirely.

To me Japan is the land of the paradox, and the idea of doing a flower arrangement without flowers is the paradox sublime. Yet that is the essence of the avant-garde style. And it is therefore possible to go to a modern flower arrangement exhibition in Japan and find not a flower in sight.

Avant-garde is really a form of sculpture, with wood, metal and stone as the main ingredients. Oddly-shaped pieces of wood might be combined with weirdly-twisted wires, or jagged pieces of rock entwined with lengths of metal tubing. The possibilities are endless and the material could be almost anything—except, of course, flowers. But even in this surrealistic style a knowledge of the basic principles of flower arrangement is important. Without an instinctive feeling for balance, proportion, contrast and harmony—all of which are absorbed in the constant practice of the basic arrangements—the newcomer to the avant-garde style can hope to create little but chaos. Form and line are no less essential than they are in any other arrangement, whatever the material or the style.

Avant-garde arrangements are not, of course, to everyone's taste and have caused as much controversy as their counterparts in the world of art. Nevertheless, when

33 An avant-garde *shikibana* arrangement with clear plastic solids and gladiolus heads on a black base (*see p. 99*)

the eye has become accustomed to them, they can have a very strong appeal and a kind of beauty. When done on a small scale they can make superlative table decorations. Plate 99 is an example illustrating a *haiku* (p. 162).

In the sections that follow, you will see that these styles have been variously used, and you should have no trouble in picking out which style is which. Of course, basic *moribana* and *nageire* styles can be used where you might be inspired in that direction. There is no rule to say that the old and the new cannot be mixed, that once you have mastered the fundamental styles you will no longer make basic arrangements. The only point I would reiterate is that you should not attempt advanced arrangements until you have thoroughly acquainted yourself with the fundamental ones.

You should have no difficulty in understanding what each of the following arrangements is attempting to illustrate, and I hope you will be encouraged to set about creating your own solution to the problems posed here.

34 Giant clam shells with pink roses

DIFFERENT KINDS OF MATERIALS

SEASHELLS
The shells in this arrangement are Australian giant clams, worn down by the sun and sea but still strong; they are used with the delicate Queen Elizabeth rose. The effect is the contrast of the durable and the fragile. You might try another way of using this material, or, indeed, see this arrangement in an entirely different light. It is very personal, and yet when the arrangement is done skilfully, it strikes a chord of universal and eternal truth recognizable by all. The bottle-green vase enhances both the strength and the fragility of the arrangement and gives a feeling of coolness as in early summer. If another rose were added, the subtle sense of contrast would be lost.

THE COMBINATION OF DIFFERENT MATERIALS
In this arrangement, a gerbera, a fatsia leaf, a hoop of cane and a branch of palm flying out in front of the cane all

work together to create a sense of great speed. These
materials are anchored in a black pot, itself established on
a polished wood base. The base and the pot keep the
arrangement from taking off altogether. The effect is racy,
sunny, bright, fresh, happy, youthful and gay.

SPRAYED WOOD

Willow tortuoso sprayed with quick-drying gold paint is
combined here with two roses and privet leaves to create
the contrast, as well as the balance, for a square, ceramic
pot which could also be regarded as a difficult one. The
willow is placed in a vertical position in order to draw the
eye away from the weight of the container. Ordinarily the
willow is just stripped and used in its natural colour state.
Here gold paint highlights the branch and gives it some
substance, as on its own the branch is too thin to hold the
arrangement together. Spraying wood—or other objects
and materials—is just another way of enhancing an

36 Gilded wood with pink roses and
privet leaves

arrangement, and, as in this case, showing off the
marvellous roses. When it is a good year for roses, it is a
pity not to use them in as many different ways as possible:
they always evoke restfulness and well-being.

MORIMONO
This is an arrangement either in a shallow dish or on a
base, using fruit in place of the flowers and extremely
short plant material. They are combined with careful
consideration of the shapes and colours of the fruits and
other materials to create the effect of a still-life painting.
In Plate 23 (p. 65) persimmons and green grapes are
combined. Any fruit can be used, although you are
better off with smaller fruit as this is really meant to be an
intimate table arrangement. But you must guard against
eating it!

37 An unusual ceramic container
with yellow freesia and dried
seaweed

UNUSUAL CONTAINERS

BASKETS

Open baskets would seem to suggest a moon arrangement, a single basket set upright, the flowers and
branches secured in a well *kenzan* behind it. However,
three baskets have been used here, and it is the piling up
of the baskets, the flowers poking through them, that
makes this so striking (Plate 31, p. 85).

To complement the Enchantment lilies the background
is a rose-orange. This brings out the bright orange of the
lilies and their deep green leaves. You will notice that no
base has been included here: if you use baskets you do
not need one.

THE SIDE-OPENING CERAMIC CONTAINER

We all have vases or containers in our homes that have
lived on top shelves or in the back of a cupboard for a
number of years because we could never imagine how
they might be used. Before you are tempted to dispose of

38 A patterned ceramic bowl with
a blush camellia and viburnum

such a vase or bowl, have another look at it and see if it
provides a stimulus to your skills in ikebana. Think how
you might be able to tranform the container by combin-
ing it with other unusual materials, or very ordinary
materials, into something quite startling and unexpected.

Here seaweed and freesia are placed in this awkward
vase. The opening of the vase is small and set on one side.
At first glance it would seem impossible to do anything
with it. But once you have risen to the challenge posed by
a container like this, you will find yourself looking out for
similar containers and materials. You must, though, think
about the arrangement first, not the unusual material.
After placing the seaweed, you carefully arrange the
freesia. Then, once the container is positioned on a
lacquer base, you find that the problem has been
successfully overcome.

THE GLASS CONTAINER

Modern glass vases and bowls are very much to the
forefront in the shops, especially exquisite hand-blown
creations which do not seem to lend themselves to
flower-arranging. They do not have much room for
flowers, let alone flowers and branches. Here are two
lovely pieces of glass brought together by bleached, dried
branches, resting on a wooden base and set off by the
dahlias in the one vase. There is just room for the flowers.
This arrangement would go very well on a modern dinner-
table as a centre-piece. It would also look well in a
conversational setting on a round table (Plate 32, p.87).

THE PATTERNED CERAMIC BOWL

This illustrates the use of a tricky container as well as what
might be called a difficult lighting problem. This arrangement can be placed in a hallway where there is no direct
light, and yet there is enough to permit its outlines to be
seen, provided that pale material forms its substance.

Here a white camellia is used with a budding viburnum
branch. The ceramic container's design provides a subtle
contrast with the whiteness of the camellia. A difficult
container like this, as I have said often before, challenges
you to make the most of it.

A SWIFT-SAILING BOAT

There are many ways in which this type of container can
be used—as an incoming or outgoing boat, a boat at

39 A patio arrangement using a
variety of tall containers with breeze
blocks, glass balls and hydrangeas

anchor or a swift-sailing one. In the first, there will be
several flowers representing a full cargo. They could be
fish or could be sandalwood—anything that comes to
your mind. The outgoing boat will have fewer flowers, and
they will be small ones which suggest its lightness. The
boat at anchor will be put on a base and the branches and
leaves will be close together, pointing skyward, to suggest
stillness. Plate 30 shows the swift-sailing boat (p. 83).
The branches are bent as though in a high wind. The
carnations represent the passengers and the crew.

You will have to be very careful when you bend your
branch as you want an exaggerated line. You might be
lucky, however, and find such a branch growing in just
this sort of curve, so be sure to have a good look for your
material first.

FREE-STANDING ARRANGEMENTS

OUTDOOR ARRANGEMENT

A free-standing arrangement is one that you can see from
all sides and that you can walk around. It is not often that

40 Driftwood with mahonia and japonica

building materials are available or are even remotely associated in the mind's eye with an arrangement. But here they provided the inspiration. To heighten the effect, five tall ceramic containers have been used. The hydrangeas and the coloured glass balls provide the contrast to the straight lines of the pots and the breeze blocks. Dried eucalyptus leaves tie the different parts of the arrangement together. This is the sort of arrangement you might do for your patio or in your garden.

DRIFTWOOD
Driftwood is a generic term covering any pieces of bare, dried wood. It could be a root, a tree stump, branches, stripped willow—anything that to your mind fits the category. When you pile it up and try to gain balance as well as height, extraordinarily abstract designs occur. It can be great fun experimenting with different structures, so enjoyable, in fact, that you may decide to leave your creation unadorned as an avant-garde wood sculpture. But adding branches and flowers can be part of the design as well. Here mahonia and japonica are woven into the driftwood fabric.

NO CONTAINER

LEAVES AND FLOWERS

This arrangement is done with agapanthus and fatsia leaves. The leaves and the blossoms are secured in a well *kenzan* filled with water so that the materials will stay fresh for some time.

It is possible to arrange an endless number of materials in this way. While no container is needed, a base is necessary in order to give stability to the arrangement. It is the sort of arrangement you can do when you find yourself without a container, or when the only containers available are unsuitable for what you would like to do. You can create your arrangement with the material at hand and use as a base perhaps a pastry board, a chopping-board or a flat stone slab—anything that catches your eye. If you are visiting friends your no-container arrangement will be a delightful and welcome gesture of appreciation for their hospitality.

41 *Above* Fatsia leaves and agapanthus flowers arranged without a container on a black base

42 A large root used with bronze chrysanthemums and oak leaves

ROOTS

There are a myriad ways of arranging materials without a container. A walk through the countryside in autumn is often a source of inspiration. A hefty root, like the one used here, or an oak branch are among the items you might bring home with you and combine, as has been done here, with bronze spray chrysanthemums. The root on its own is rather plain and uninteresting, so a sheet of copper has been nailed to the underside to give it a reflective quality. This piece of wood can be used in any position. Here it seems to counter-balance the chrysanthemums and the oak leaves.

PIECES OF GLASS OR PLASTIC

You may not have pieces of clear glass (or bits of extruded plastic materials, for that matter) in your home, but you should be able to locate a manufacturer who, for a small consideration, would be willing to part with some. The sizes will vary, and what sizes you use will depend on your judgement. Some very large chunks of glass can be produced, but it is wiser to obtain a number of small ones which can be combined with some floral material rather than get out a hammer and do the job yourself.

Tubes of extruded plastic have been put with green orchids to create a very delicate feeling. They are set on a black base which shows off the orchids and the plastic forms to full advantage (Plate 2, p. 11).

SHIKIBANA

Shikibana is an arrangement which stands on a table without a container and without a *kenzan*. You might describe this as a thrown-on-the-table arrangement. If you create a *shikibana* for a dinner-party, you will have to dismantle it as soon as you finish eating. A variety of materials can be used for it. In the arrangement on p. 89 (Plate 33), clear plastic cubes, triangles and rectangles are used with gladiolus heads on black plexiglass bases, one of which is raised. The flowers are used here not as flowers but as abstract elements.

A *shikibana* is a splendid opportunity for serendipity, especially when you are clearing your garden in spring and autumn. Dried leaves and dead branches that you would otherwise throw away can be transformed.

CHAPTER VII

SEASONAL ARRANGEMENTS

You have now some familiarity both with fundamental styles and with advanced arrangements in which the traditional symbolism of heaven, man and earth is forsaken and anything that strikes the imagination can be expressed. It might seem as if, having offered such freedom, I am now imposing fresh limitations by introducing the theme of seasonal arrangements. But this is not so, for you will find that having a theme is a double challenge to creativity. Not only do you have to attune your innermost self to the seasonal mood you wish to convey, you must also find appropriate material. In effect, you are quite free to do exactly as you wish.

Initially you might feel that it would be possible to do only one arrangement for each season – one that would sum it up, so to speak. Here I have given you eight for each season, and there are any number of refinements. I have said very little about the arrangements in the hope that you can study and discover for yourself the feeling behind each. As you go more deeply into the subject your intuition will come to the fore, so that you will find yourself engaged in silent meditation while making an ikebana arrangement. The thoughts that occur to you will be more poetic than discursive:

Hundreds of spring flowers, the autumnal moon,
A refreshing summer breeze, winter snow –
Free thy mind from idle thoughts,
For thee how enjoyable every season is!

Mumon

SPRING

THE EVENING BREEZE IN SPRING
'When the wind blows, everything that can be shaken is shaken. And even those things which do not tremble feel the force and power of it. When something happens, it happens to everything. As for the roses, every one sways and tosses and trembles. All are the same in moving, though all are different in their movement. To express it

43 A summer shower: Japanese iris seed-heads, dried branch with gypsophila and hydrangea (see p. 111)

44 The evening breeze in spring: cane and a rose in a square vase

more simply and too profoundly for the intellect to fathom, all are the same, because all are different.' Reginald Blyth provides the perfect verbal illustration for the feeling this arrangement evokes. You can easily imagine a bed of roses, the one rose here standing for the multitude. The cane and even the hole in the vase suggest the penetrating motion of the wind. And yet they do not move in the same way that the rose moves.

APRIL MOON
The moon here is a waxing or new moon. In the spring the appearance of the moon in the night sky heralds good weather. The japonica (or chaenomeles, as it is properly called) is placed in the centre of the moon in this arrangement with an upright budding branch extending beyond the moon container. The air is crystal clear and slightly chill. The japonica seems to be standing at attention, alert, as if listening for sounds of life. All activity appears to have ceased. Nature is resting. But if you listen in rapt silence, you may hear the buds opening.

45 April moon: japonica in a moon container

There are two other 'moons', so to speak – the full moon and the waning. The placement of the branch indicates which moon you are depicting. In the full moon arrangement, the branch and flowers must be enclosed in the centre space. For the waning moon, the branch flows downward beyond the container's edge.

THE STIRRING OF SPRING

You usually think of daffodils in great profusion, gently nodding in unison, stirring a delighted response in the onlooker. Here only a handful of daffodils have been used to symbolize the stirring of spring. Both the evergreen mahonia and the ever yellow daffodils are reflected in the water, which is perfectly clear. The only movement is in the buds as they obey their own nature and open to the warming April sun.

The budding daffodils also represent the beginning of all life. The very thought of life beginning is a joyous one, and at the same time fills you with awe that something so simple and so inevitable is taking place before your eyes. You are reminded that your own life opens and can

46 The stirring of spring: daffodils and mahonia in two containers, one shallow and one tall

47 The quiet beginnings of spring: willow, blue iris and wild arum

unfold according to its true nature, provided that you are mindful and self-possessed. The daffodils seem to communicate that it is right to be true to your own self.

THE QUIET BEGINNINGS OF SPRING

A budding strand of willow suspended over the water seems to be silently calling the iris into life. All nature is rejoicing as the winter snows recede, as the sun warms the earth and encourages everything to grow and flourish. This experience gives a perception of the destiny of life: the mind grows attuned to the truth in the impersonal and quite normal process of seasonal change. The willow will burst into leaf, the iris will rise majestically from the stream whether they are observed or not, spring after spring after spring.

MISTY SPRING

While you may not be able to see the tree in the early morning mist, the fragrance of the mimosa is overpowering. The fragrance seems to linger even as the mist clears

away, but you cannot stand there for long drinking it in. A momentary experience encapsulates the eternal.

Very little mimosa is needed here. Other fragrant flowers can be used, but always in small amounts so that the scent does not overwhelm.

From what flowering tree
I know not—
But ah, the fragrance!   Basho

THE VITALITY OF SPRING

The tulip originally came from Turkey and is not a native European flower, although it was imported into Holland and has been associated with the Dutch for many centuries. Tulips have not until recently been strong enough to use in an ikebana arrangement. Now they are so hardy that an arrangement of tulips on their own—that is, the blooms and the leaves—is most satisfactory.

Here they are being used to illustrate the vitality of spring. This is the most important element of new growth,

48 *Far left* Misty spring: mimosa
with willow tortuoso and white iris

49 *Left* The vitality of spring: tulip
flowers and leaves with gold-
sprayed split bamboo, in a
container designed by Hiroshi
Teshigahara

50 Hidden spring: violets and
hornbeam with ferns and day-lily
shoots on slate

for without inherent vitality nothing survives. The sun and
soil and moisture nourish the new plants and the world is
transformed. But the vital centre is silently realizing its
own nature, as the tulip unfolds towards the sun. Do not
forget when arranging tulips to use the leaves and make
the most of them.

HIDDEN SPRING

A violet by a mossy stone
Half hidden from the eye

Reginald Blyth uses this couplet to give a picture familiar
in spring when violets seem to appear out of nowhere in
every country wood. Violets have so many associations
and meanings that it would be impossible to list them all.
This arrangement attempts to convey the feeling that
something small is also significant. You really have to
contemplate the violet at close quarters; you then find
yourself drawn into a mysterious, unseen world, which
you discover is the world of your own mind.

51 The evanescence of spring: yellow freesia and gypsophila in glass vases

THE EVANESCENCE OF SPRING

Just as we are beginning to enjoy the new life and new growth of spring, it seems to disappear overnight and summer is upon us. Here we feel the quickly fading nature of spring in the minute flowers of the gypsophila. Arranged with yellow freesia, they seem to be but pinpoints, remnants of a former self, in contrast to the more substantial freesia. One of the slender purple glass vases stands on a purple base, while the other rests on black containers in turn reflected in the base. This enhances the feeling of insubstantiality of the floral material. The arrangement echoes Kito's poem:

While I slumbered
Overwearied,
Spring drew to its close

52 Summer bounty: hydrangeas in a celadon vase with driftwood on a wooden base

SUMMER

SUMMER BOUNTY

The sight of enormous hydrangea bushes in the summer garden gives the same impact as the sight of rhododendron bushes in the spring. This effect is recreated here with the combination of driftwood and hydrangea blooms. The driftwood is massive and strong, providing a stark complement to a spray of nine delicately pink hydrangeas. It is not usual to use so many flowers, but fewer in this arrangement would have meant that the balance demanded by the massed driftwood would not have been achieved. The hydrangeas are not placed in the driftwood but in a celadon ceramic vase that fits behind the wood. This gives the right height for balance, as well as blending with the material. You need to think

53 On a summer evening: clematis and hosta leaves in a glass vase by Anthony Stern

very carefully about the sort of container you use with random pieces of wood: it needs to perform a number of tasks while at the same time remaining unobtrusive.

A SUMMER SHOWER

The rain in summer can be soft or torrential: you never know when you look skyward at lowering clouds what they will bring. But whether the rain is gentle or severe, all growing things will be refreshed by it.

The shower illustrated on p. 101 (Plate 43) is of the gentle variety, punctuated by gusts of strong wind, the gypsophila representing the steady fall of rain, the stalks of iris giving the feeling of the force of the wind. The dark clouds are still threatening, as indicated by a dark background and a black vase. The tiny pool of white pebbles at the base of the vase accentuates the constancy of the falling rain.

ON A SUMMER EVENING

The evening summer sky is often a glorious sequence of changing hues ranging from pale yellow to deep purple. The deeper tones are reminiscent of the sun setting behind a mountain range. Even though a cool breeze begins to stir as the sky grows darker, the evening casts such a spell that the spectator is reluctant to retreat inside.

This is the feeling captured by this arrangement. Varying tones of purple are blended to suggest the end of the day, in the clematis, the hand-blown glass vase and the deep purple base on which the arrangement stands.

A HOT SUMMER'S DAY

This arrangement suggests high summer, mid-July, when the poppies have bloomed and fallen and the geraniums are at their most dazzling. The air is so clear that the lines and the colours stand out as if etched on the horizon.

Bending two of the poppy heads sharply alters the vertical direction established by the others, so giving a dynamism to the space around the geraniums. This movement echoes the pattern on the container.

By partially hiding one of the geraniums you can bring out the beauty of the leaves, which most people do not ordinarily appreciate. This too creates something of an electrical field, as it were, although it is much subtler than that of the pointing poppies. With so much activity going

on above it, the heaviness of the container becomes an asset. It is set off by the red-green polarization of the geraniums.

MIDSUMMER HARVEST

With the first cutting of the corn, you realize that midsummer has begun. Up to this point, the growing, waving wheat has been taken for granted. It is not until it has been cut down that any deeper understanding of the workings of nature comes to you. The eternal cycle of birth, life and death is symbolized in this arrangement by sheaves of wheat, an hibiscus leaf and the delicate mauve yarrow. These are placed in a well *kenzan* in an equally delicate basket of bamboo set on its side.

THE FRUITS OF SUMMER

When you think of the fruits of summer, you think of strawberries, raspberries, red- and black-currants or gooseberries. However, these would not last very long in a flower arrangement. Here, to suggest the fruits of summer, japonica and hydrangea in a hand-blown glass bowl set

54 *Far left* A hot summer's day: poppy seed-heads and geraniums in a ceramic container

55 *Left* Midsummer harvest: wheat-sheaves, hibiscus leaf and yarrow with two bamboo baskets

57 The fruits of summer: japonica with apples and hydrangea in a glass bowl by Anthony Stern

off the apples in this arrangement. The hydrangea picks up the hint of pink in the apples. The apple leaves are still green, but the fruit may drop at any moment. Using a turquoise bowl is an unexpected touch, as is the grey slate base. These seem to hold the otherwise flyaway branches, and the apples have been placed to cast a shadow.

SULTRY AUGUST
This is the season for holidays, for indolence, for lying in the sun, an umbrella over you, enjoying your inactivity. The season inexorably proceeds through its various changes. The dahlia will hold the brightness of the late summer's heat, but the blackthorn has already passed its peak. The fatsia will remain evergreen.

THE DELICACY OF LATE SUMMER
There can be something very delicate about a late summer day, which is lovely to capture in an arrangement. Rose-hips and the last roses of summer are combined here to express the onset of autumn. Too soon

56 Sultry August: a dahlia with a fatsia leaf and blackthorn

58 The delicacy of late summer: roses and wild rose-hips in a George Wilson pot

59 A September afternoon: faded hydrangeas with sprayed driftwood

the rose petals will fall and only the rose-hips will be left in the garden. They are perhaps more beautiful than the roses themselves, although you would not be inclined to think so were the roses not there. The very slender vase gives this emphasis. A shorter container would pull the arrangement down and destroy the very fragile effect.

AUTUMN

A SEPTEMBER AFTERNOON

When the hydrangeas have lost their brilliant colours and have turned pale green, pink and mauve, and their leaves have become tinged with red, they provide the perfect

expression of a number of early autumn moods such as the musk of an autumn afternoon. The subdued colours are, in fact, more appealing. Here they stand bunched in a black and gold container, a piece of driftwood sprayed black and gold set on its edge. The arrangement can be seen from all directions, so it would be effective as a centre-piece on a low coffee-table.

IN THE MOUNTAINS IN AUTUMN
Pine forests cover the mountains, giving them substance and majesty. The bleached weeping mulberry accentuates the evergreen pine branches and reinforces the idea of substantiality and endurance. You could be walking up a mountain path, and turn a corner to find a branch

bleached by the sun standing out against the pine. The green-mauve hydrangeas enhance the feeling of being deep in the forest. By placing the arrangement in a tall ceramic pot, you convey the feeling that the forest density can be penetrated, so you can confidently continue on your way up the mountain path.

THE LUSHNESS OF AUTUMN

This arrangement combines green beech, vine and breeze blocks to suggest the beginning of autumn. The wind has whipped the branch from a tree and it has become entangled with the dry vine. The neutral colour of the breeze blocks set in and around the beech and vine plays up the green leaves, which are mellowing into gold. At any moment you feel that the wind may rise again, scattering the fallen leaves and carrying the entangled branch and vine away; but the solidity of the breeze blocks will somehow prevent the wind from doing too much damage (Plate 4, p. 12).

60 *Far left* In the mountains in autumn: stripped weeping mulberry, pine and hydrangeas in a pot by Phil Sherwood

61 *Left* Falling leaves of autumn: rue leaves and bronze chrysanthemums in a William Quick pot, with two unpainted wooden gates used as a base

62 The fading passion of autumn: brushwood and passion-flower fruit in a double vase by Ivy Denner

FALLING LEAVES OF AUTUMN

This arrangement gives the impression that the sun has just come up and the leaves that have fallen in the night have not yet blown away. The dew, however, has gone: the sun is welcoming you warmly. Rue branches, their bare tips reaching towards the sun's warmth, hide spray chrysanthemums, and are themselves set off by bleached wooden gates. You might have expected black lacquer gates: but then the effect would have been sombre. The lighter wood against the dark amber glaze of the vase energizes the variegated tones of the leaves and flowers.

THE FADING PASSION OF AUTUMN

As soon as passion arises it will fade away. Here skeleton brushwood meshes with passion-flower vines on which five fruits have ripened, soon to fall. All hope is not lost, however; the vine is still vigorous, and the seeds of the fruit promise new life. Only the lichen-covered branches seem to declare a certain finality.

AN AUTUMN BREEZE

The breeze just starting to stir the green beech leaves – barely beginning to turn yellow-gold – hints at an autumn storm. White Fuji chrysanthemums seem to tremble: there is nowhere to shelter from the impending tempest. The coming rain could turn to sleet, and their delicate petals would then wither and fall. You will notice that the arrangement stands in a copper container, which suggests moisture, and is set off by a small root.

LATE AUTUMN TWILIGHT

This much more formal arrangement of oak leaves and three single gold chrysanthemums catches the late autumn sun in such a way that its final rays seem like snowflakes. Winter is almost here. You are at once enchanted by the rich blaze of light and saddened by the thought of the approaching bleakness. The root has been

63 *Far left* An autumn breeze: Fuji chrysanthemums and beech leaves in a copper bowl, with a bleached root

64 *Left* Late autumn twilight: oak leaves and large chrysanthemums in a ceramic pot

added to balance the weight of the flowers. The tall pot gives the arrangement a feeling of elegance and grandeur.

65 The chill of autumn: Jerusalem sage seed-pods and flowering currant with pieces of wood, metal bolts and hinges

THE CHILL OF AUTUMN

Reginald Blyth said, 'The cold of winter is somewhat different from that of autumn, the former being perhaps more physical, the latter more spiritual.'

Here autumn chill is conveyed by Jerusalem sage seed-pods and flowering currant arranged with weatherbeaten pieces of wooden posts, rusty hinges and bolts. There is no light. Only the silhouettes of the pods and branches appear against a September sky. It is night and it is cold, but you do not shudder or shiver. The leaves have not yet all dropped off the branches. When that happens, you will feel the cold intensely. But now you are content to experience the peace of this night, to be a part of it and let it absorb you.

WINTER

A WINTER'S MOON

The light of a winter's moon is a clear, cold white. It illuminates the pure calm of midnight. Nothing moves. Nature's work is apparently done, at least in so far as any visible manifestations are concerned. But while the world sleeps under the impersonal gaze of the moon, there are minute stirrings of new life as seen in the lighter green tips of the pine. In this arrangement depicting the full moon, the flowers and branches are all contained in its centre. The white chrysanthemums symbolize the brightness of the moon in a cloudless sky.

WINTER FOG

When the fog comes down on a winter's day, it so envelops everything that you find yourself without

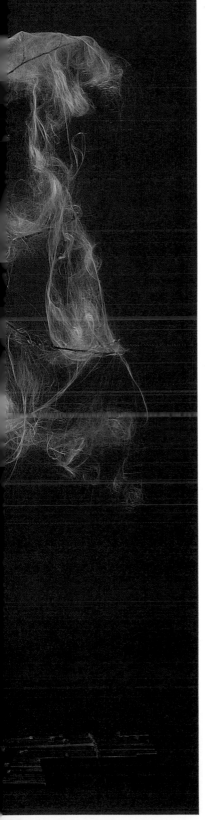

66 *Far left* A winter's moon: white chrysanthemums and pine branches in a moon container

67 *Left* Winter fog: gypsophila and white chrysanthemum with senecio, hornbeam, driftwood, and angel hair

68 *Right* Chill winter sun: Chinese lanterns and iris seed-pods with dried elder and pine branches

bearings. The landmarks are still where they always were, but not being able to see them robs them of their usefulness. You feel, when it initially settles, that the fog will never lift. But as with all phenomena, this, too, will pass.

The hornbeam, protruding through the moss-covered thorn, promises that the fog will go. How soon you cannot tell, but the ray of hope is there.

CHILL WINTER SUN

All nature sparkles in the chill winter sun; the weather is crisp and clear and very, very cold. Although the sun shines, there is no warmth in it. A robin alights on a fence-post and thence to the ground, busily searching for crumbs. You can imagine the robin scurrying around the Chinese lanterns, darting behind the seed-pods, hopping on to the branch to survey his kingdom. In a flash he will be gone, but the sun will remain and the bird may return.

69 The first snow: a log of silver
birch with snowdrops

70 The new year dawns: white
orchids, dried Japanese vine and
pine branches

THE FIRST SNOW

The first snow usually melts as soon as it falls, leaving everything more or less just as it was. The temperature, which had dropped with the approaching flurries, rises very slightly, but will fall again, just as the snow-laden clouds will pass overhead again. You might feel downcast at the prospect of increasingly colder weather and, eventually, an enduring coat of white. With the snow on the ground you can hear for miles; the first snow provides no such dampening blanket. Rather, all sound seems to be caught in the snowdrops.

THE NEW YEAR DAWNS

You might expect the New Year to coincide with a change in the weather, but it does not. The wind is still bitter, and any movement on the ground or on the tips of the branches is quickly stilled by the biting cold. But new life is stirring and will slowly but surely come into blossom. And while you have resolved to begin anew, to try this year to turn over a new leaf, there is nothing inevitable about your resolve. However, it is time to be bright and hopeful as well as positive and inwardly confident that you will be equal to the tasks you have set for yourself. The bright orchids would counteract the grey sameness of winter and contribute to your enthusiasm.

WINTER'S WIND

The winter wind has a song all its own, one that enchants and repels at the same time. It seems to call the fox from his den and urge him to cross the empty fields, warily, for the wind's song tells him to keep a look-out for a hunter, or small boys with slings. The fields seem to have been scraped clean by the wind, little tufts of dried grasses being tossed to and fro, defenceless, always moving with the wind as if willing their own destruction—yet they do not die.

WITHERED BRANCHES

The view through the forest in winter does not seem so bleak and barren when broken by tangles of bare branches. You can still see the horizon, but it is not so stark. Although the leaves have fallen and the branches are, to all intents and purposes, dead, their interference, as it were, softens the impact of winter. Dark against light, their tiny twigs rigid against the twilight sky hold the horizon in its place.

71 *Far left* Winter's wind: hellebore and heather root with driftwood on a slate base

72 *Left* Withered branches: blackthorn and mahonia with a yellow lily

73 *Above* Winter garden: hellebore and rose-hips with cupressus, prunus branches and driftwood

WINTER GARDEN

The garden in winter is desolate indeed. The only movement is that of the sparrows hopping about, seemingly unafraid of human presence as they search for seeds. Apart from their chattering, no sound is to be heard. A distant wisp of smoke indicates that the fire has been lit but the scent of burning yew will never reach the garden: a scent of something would cheer the dreary tangle.

CHAPTER VIII

IKEBANA AS A WAY OF LIFE

In this final chapter there are three topics which go beyond the mechanics of arranging flowers (or, as in the case of abstract or avant-garde arrangements, arranging anything you choose). In the previous chapter, 'Seasonal Arrangements', I attempted to show you that you can capture the spirit of seasonal changes in your ikebana. Now I want to look at what I regard as very personal modes of interpretation, and this is why I have called this chapter 'Ikebana as a Way of Life'.

I cannot say too often or too emphatically that the key to success with your ikebana is practice. It is only through continued practice that you are able to acquire more than a nodding acquaintance with the true nature of your materials and how they behave in certain conditions. With continuous practice you will ultimately experience mental and physical well-being, a deep respect for nature and for your fellow men and women, a diminishing of the ego and the growth inside yourself of a spiritual sense, a tranquil attitude and an abiding gentleness of character. These attributes will come out in your arrangements quite naturally, as through your practice they become part of your own nature. Rather, I should say, through your practice of ikebana the qualities which are your basic nature, your real self, underneath layers of conditioning, will rise to the surface. And they will be apparent in all of your other activities, your words, thoughts and feelings as well.

In the introduction something has been said of the relationship between ikebana and Buddhist principles and practices. The words 'Buddhist' and 'Zen' need not put you off. They are foreign only in so far as there is no need to understand anything about them until you begin to take up an eastern interest or art. But the easterner, the Japanese in particular, looks upon any artistic expression as the form of the formless. Through the practice of an art, such as ikebana, you reach beyond mere outward appearances to ultimate reality. But you get only a momentary glimpse: the repeated practice of expression of eternal truths, of personal feelings, of a poetic

74 Fill up the well with snow: gypsophila and white Japanese tulip on driftwood (*see p. 136*)

interpretation gives you increasingly greater insight into that which is beyond words or expression.

To help you understand more clearly some of the more fundamental ideas explored here, let me suggest that you look at any of the works of D. T. Suzuki and Alan W. Watts. These writers are well known in the west and, I feel, the most sympathetic to the expression of Buddhist principles in art forms. Both Dr Suzuki and Alan Watts were regular visitors to the Buddhist Society in London where I attended a Zen class for many years. It was given by the late Christmas Humphries, who himself provided me with deep insight into the Buddha's teachings. I would also like to mention Phiroz Mehta, who still gives his inspiring talks there. Any one of the various books he has written is invaluable in understanding the broader philosophical themes.

There are many excellent books on the subject, of course. The important thing is to begin to familiarize yourself with Buddhist thought and its special development in Japan through the Zen school.

The subjects presented in this chapter under three headings are the types of assignment I give to advanced students. Often such a theme will also be the subject of the talk given at the monthly meeting of the London Sogetsu Branch. Students are asked to find material which relates to the topic, and to share their interpretation with the rest of the group. Then they go on to make their arrangements. At our Sogetsu meeting, we make arrangements based on the talk given the previous month, so we have plenty of time to reflect on what we will do. Students and friends are most enthusiastic about this approach to ikebana, as it requires them to reach beyond an ordinary, everyday understanding of the world and calls up some deep, universal spiritual response.

I encourage you, then, simply to let go of your cares and put aside any preconceived notions about what you find in front of you—words or pictures: allow your intuitive mind to 'see' and understand. And I invite you to explore the uncharted fields of your own mind and heart to try and express those things which are most personal to you. Remember that, while others will see your arrangement, it is yours, the result of your attentive and careful efforts as well as your innermost thoughts and feelings. So you are perfectly free to do whatever you wish.

75 The unseen bridge: white hydrangea, iris leaves and a black basket

PHILOSOPHICAL THEMES

I have given you quite a few of these themes because you will find making your own arrangements to them both challenging and exciting. Each requires some time for thought as well as execution, for you are going to become the connecting link between the known world and the unknown. The way to proceed is to let your insight guide you. You want a direct, non-analytic expression of the theme in the simplest terms possible, so that as you are working your intuition keeps constantly informing your actions. The resulting arrangement will then be an explicit statement of the implicit. Continued practice of these themes is the only way to understand fully what I am trying to suggest and what it means to illustrate such a theme through ikebana.

There is no set order to these themes. Certainly you need not feel that you must start with the first and struggle through to the last. It is essential that you concentrate your efforts on the task at hand and forget about the applause that might accrue to you for having done an arrangement of this sort. Remember that you are but the instrument, the channel between the known and the unknown; in order that the energy flows freely through you, you will need to forget yourself, your ego.

THE UNSEEN BRIDGE

Crossing the unseen bridge is the means by which we go from the known world to the unknowable. In Zen teaching this is another way of saying that it is only possible to understand something by transcending it. The act of transcendence is an act of intuition in which there is no individual personality. Subject and object merge into one absolute emptiness.

In coming to ikebana we are carried across the unseen bridge. We are giving a transient, tangible expression to a timeless, spaceless truth, and we are doing it by activating our intuition.

Crossing the unseen bridge is expressed in this arrangement by the visible closer end of the bridge, the two white hydrangeas and the overhanging iris leaves. But the other end of the bridge is not seen by the naked eye. However, intuitively we know that it is there and that in crossing it we are never really crossing it as there is nowhere to go. The inner spirit connects with the outer spirit as they are

76 The utility of futility: gladioli and seaweed with scrap-iron

of the same nature. We cross the bridge with every insight into things as they really are.

THE UTILITY OF FUTILITY
'All men know the utility of useful things, but they do not know the utility of futility', Chuang-tse says of Lao-tse's aphorism on the Futility of Contention. This is the teaching of the 'way' or the *Tao* in Chinese (*Do* in Japanese). Ikebana is one of the Ways to True Wisdom; therefore to contemplate and then intuitively understand the Utility of Futility—and its reverse, the Futility of Utility—is to plumb the depths of one's own being.

Essentially all things are one. This paradox points to the eternal truth of constant change. A spanner that has outlived its mechanical usefulness and has been thrown

77 The futility of utility: hydrangea and driftwood with a fishnet

away, a rusted container that is no longer of any use serve the functions of support. By the same token, a collection of dried roots and two strands of dried seaweed are useless as far as their original intent is concerned: yet they form the basis for this arrangement while the gladiolus buds burst into bloom and fade away. The wooden base, worn by the sea, also served a useful purpose once. Individually each of these items appears to have no value whatsoever. Combined, they cease to be what they originally were and come full circle in terms of the Utility of Futility.

THE FUTILITY OF UTILITY
Catching a hydrangea head in a fishnet is the epitome of the Futility of Utility. Correctly speaking, the fishnet

should be horizontal, in the water, its open end held against the incoming current. Here it is supported on a piece of driftwood. The leaves of the hydrangea separate from the flower, and have no use at all. What more can be said?

THE UNCONDITIONED STATE OF SEARCH

Phiroz Mehta has said, 'The way of the world is the way of grasping. Whatever I grasp is deprived of the freedom of life, becomes corpse-like and in turn clutches me as if with ghost-tentacles.' It is necessary first to die to the way of the world if you are to search earnestly and diligently for the truth. The process of learning is then a process of opening your heart and your mind to all experiences, for experience is the only teacher of true wisdom. This involves attachment to no thing—nothing.

The unconditioned state of search is a state in which you, the searcher, welcome each new day and whatever it brings with gladness. You live fully in the moment, without choosing, without judging, without accepting, without rejecting. In this arrangement the roses represent the searcher, the lichen-covered hawthorn the way which has been trodden but has been given up. However, it still stretches its 'ghost-tentacles' towards the searcher who, living in the here and now, is not touched. The state of purification that is achieved provides the motivation for the continued search, aware, attuned and perceptive.

EMERGENCE INTO THE SILENCE

The Zen tradition speaks of communicating the *Dharma*, or Law—the teachings of the Buddha—as a transmission from mind to mind: no words are spoken; it is a transaction which occurs in silence. When two people experience that silence simultaneously, they communicate with each other in a language without words, without grammar. Therefore there is no chance of misunderstanding.

No amount of philosophical debate or argument over the meaning of words brings us any closer to the point of emergence into the silence. The practice of rapt attention to whatever it is we are doing prepares us for this entry, for it is impossible to be fully absorbed and mentally distracted at the same time. Full attention is silent attention. It is the only way to learn and then to communicate what we have learned.

78 The unconditioned state of search: pink roses and lichen-covered hawthorn in a Phil Sherwood ceramic bowl

79 Emergence into the silence: white coral with arum leaves on a stone base

80 Stilling the wave of thought and feeling: leaves of iris, arum and hosta with alchemilla in two containers

STILLING THE WAVE OF THOUGHT AND FEELING

The mind has variously been described as a grasshopper, a traffic jam, a babbling brook. It can be in constant motion even when we are asleep. Thoughts and feelings come and go in what seem often to be random patterns. But the mind must be stilled before we can begin to come close to any real understanding of what it really is. Through meditation the mind becomes calm and clear as a pool of spring water. Nothing disturbs its surface; neither thoughts nor feelings well up.

This state is not permanent, however. The slightest breeze, a stone cast into the pool will shatter its mirror-like surface and the waves will again radiate outwards. The feelings and thoughts are there, beneath the surface, ready to arise at the slightest disturbance. Only full enlightenment will still the mind completely.

THE BEGINNINGLESS BEGINNING

Dr D. T. Suzuki wrote, 'The beginning of creation was a beginningless beginning, and there is a continuous timeless creation.' He is trying to say that there is no point thinking about which came first or who created what. You must simply accept what is. You *are*. It is thinking about who you are or what you are that prevents you from seeing inwardly that you are. When you see with your inward eye that you are and that the world is beginning again and again, you are enlightened. No flash of light or clap of thunder or heavenly chorus accompanies this. You simply see things directly for what they are. And this is a very humbling experience indeed.

81 The beginningless beginning: glass chunks and silver-covered plastic wire in three black plastic containers

82 *Left* The timeless communion of the nameless unknown: agapanthus with driftwood on a stone base

FILL UP THE WELL WITH SNOW

Filling up the well with snow is like catching a catfish in a gourd, holding a spade in your empty hands, passing over a bridge which flows instead of the water, walking on foot while riding on the back of an ox. Your everyday mind says that all of these things are crazy, impossible. But the ordinary way of looking at things is not the final one. If you really want to get to the bottom of life and fill up the well with snow, you have to abandon your old way of reasoning and acquire a new way of seeing which escapes the tyranny of logic and dichotomies (Plate 74, p. 127).

THE TIMELESS COMMUNION OF THE NAMELESS UNKNOWN

Timelessness and namelessness related to communion and the unknown: there is no logical or rational way of dealing with such a subject. But seeing into the true nature of things is not a logical, rational procedure. Only the mind's inner eye perceives the timeless communion of the nameless unknown when it is entirely free from impurities. Awareness comes as a clear white light which brings reality into sharp focus. The inner eye always perceives in this way, just as what it perceives stands out in its true purity. To have this clarity of inner vision is our ultimate fulfilment.

83 The mind doors burst open: tree fungus on a tripod with tiger-lilies and dried fatsia leaves on a black base

THE MIND DOORS BURST OPEN

A sudden clash of thunder, the mind-doors burst open,
And lo, there sitteth the old man in all his homeliness.

Chao-pien

The poem refers to the moment of sudden enlightenment. The mind is in its everyday, pedestrian mode when
something (and whatever it might be is a very individual
experience) breaks that mental lock that keeps the
transcendent and the everyday separate. Suddenly there
is no separation: 'The old man', Chao-pien's familiar
phrase for Buddha-nature or the divine essence in all

84 The cloud of the unknowing: blackthorn, arum lily and dieffenbachia on a stone base

things, stands clearly before you. In fact, there has never been any barrier to understanding: only thinking made it seem that there was. Locked into our private world, we have convinced ourselves that nothing else exists. We are walking through a forest when suddenly we see a fungus growing on a tree: the mind doors burst open.

It is often repeated in Zen circles that before enlightenment the mountains are just mountains, the trees are just trees, people are just people. In the flash of enlightenment we see that all these are only appearances. They have no lasting reality. But following enlightenment, once again mountains are mountains, trees are trees and people are people. That is their Buddha-nature, no more, no less.

THE CLOUD OF THE UNKNOWING

Whatever we do or try to do starts from the unknown. The answers to the most important questions about life—why are we here? Where did we come from? Where will we go eventually?—are only to be found in the calm and stillness of meditation. We cannot know the answers as we know facts with the intellect. The cloud of the unknowing can only be dispersed if we can awaken the unclouded vision of the mind emptied of all images, illusions, delusions. It is a process that goes against our natural, logical instincts, or so we think. But once the mind is still and empty and clear, the logic of the true nature of the self communicates wordlessly.

When the mind is empty, attention glows white-hot. The mind is alert, alive, attentive, fully creative, flowing. It becomes one with the unknowing, and in so doing, experiences the ineffable joy of living in reality here and now.

COSMIC VITALITY

Cosmic vitality runs through everything, energizes everything, and is there even in the tiniest particle. It is the force behind the constant changing of the universe. It is the force that you can gather through meditation and focus in a single point of light, like a laser beam, in all your activities so that not one breath is wasted, no action done in vain. Harnessing this energy within and without, you concentrate your efforts so that you become totally absorbed in what you are doing at this moment. There is no other moment, only another potential opportunity to mobilize this vitality and be fully alive (Plate 6, p. 16).

85 Locked in the dungeon of isolative self-consciousness: purple orchid, broom and fern-leaf with driftwood

LOCKED IN THE DUNGEON OF ISOLATIVE SELF-CONSCIOUSNESS

This is a prickly situation and a familiar one. When you are occupied with your own thoughts, your own problems and worries, you have no contact with the world outside. Nothing seems to matter except what is occupying you, and yet there seems to be no solution to those worrying difficulties. This is a moment when your limitation needs to be seen as your freedom. In a split second you can recognize that the problem is the fact that you have cut yourself off, locked your mind and your heart away. With this recognition, you will know precisely what to do in order to release yourself from the dungeon.

PERCEPTION OF THE BOUNDLESS VOID

This is just another way of saying that you cannot know black until you know white. In fact, everything we have been talking about in this section is essentially the same thing. You are urged to go beyond your everyday

86 Perception of the boundless void: cane hoops and camellia in a glass vase

understanding of yourself, your world, the people in it, the events of it, to take a leap into the boundless void. You can do this only when you have great faith and at the same time great doubt. The two do not cancel each other out but polarize the field between them – polarize it and harmonize all contradictions. Letting go of the known, the comfortable, the secure, is the only route to freedom. Otherwise you remain bound up in conflicts and difficulties which seem to rob you of any power. True power is only released when the mind is very still, like the camellia.

EMOTIONAL MOODS

To give concrete expression to a thought in ikebana is indeed excitingly possible; it is just as exciting to give concrete expression to emotional moods – to feelings. It is on the emotional plane that we are at once so very individual and yet so cosmically human, and eternally so. Feelings often cannot be expressed in words and are

87 Tranquillity: willow tortuoso with white iris and day-lily shoots in a large pottery container

communicated from person to person on an intuitive level. To be fully in touch with your feelings does not mean taking your emotional pulse moment to moment: rather it requires an awareness of the moments when your own experience reflects a universal sentiment, be it joy or melancholy, fear or caution. The feeling is not unique, although your expression of it may be. Certainly an arrangement depicting an emotional state calls on your personal experiences as well as your cosmic perception. So, again, you are the connecting link between the known and the unknown, as you proceed with your arrangement on any of these moods. If you are particularly moved by any other feeling or feelings, by all means see what you can create through ikebana.

TRANQUILLITY
Tranquillity, to a modern mind, too often means an artificially induced state of passivity. By taking drugs in one form or another, you can switch off your mind and exist in a dulled, non-perceptive condition. This is not the sort of thing you would want to achieve with relation to ikebana. True tranquillity is a natural state of complete awareness, the state of the fully awakened mind which perceives everything. All thinking has been stilled so that the intuitive faculties are given full play. Even those elements in nature which seem to the intellect to be anything but quiet take on a tranquil aspect. All things become clear, even the 'reasonableness' of the inexplicable and the incomprehensible.

The iris leaves are always used in Japan for the Boys' festival (the third day of the third month) to symbolize the sword of wisdom which cuts through the veils of illusion placed by the intellect before true reality. The sword cannot be used effectively until the mind is clear and still. So the iris with its leaves represents the tranquil mind of intuitive wisdom.

TURBULENCE
Turbulence comes about when something, either in nature or in yourself, is thrown out of balance. Storms at sea, a volcanic eruption, a typhoon, tornado or cyclone come most easily to mind as signs of a disturbance in the natural order of things. Internally, this turbulence can take the form of frustration, perplexity and indecision. These may be manifested in a number of different ways—bursts

143

of anger, senseless and pointless activity, depression. There does not seem to be any way to put an end to the churning. But, eventually, like the storms, it will wear itself out, though not before wreaking havoc. When calm is restored in nature, the resulting damage may or may not be evident. In human beings, however, order is not likely to return so easily. The flotsam and jetsam of the conflict-torn mind remain on its surface for a long time after the 'storm' has passed. Only by concentrated effort can the balance be re-established (Plate 5, p. 14).

FEAR
This emotion always seems to result from the lack of a sense of security, of assurances of success in the future, and of some sort of magical protection from above that will guarantee eternal happiness. On the contrary: it is the

88 *Left* Fear: dried monkey-puzzle
leaves, pine branch and yellow lilies

89 Grasping: stripped ivy with roses
and fern leaves in two containers

cause of these desires, and the result of the failure to
recognize the impossibility of such wishes. Nothing can
give you security other than your faith in the rightness of
things as they are. This realization is also your assurance of
the future (in which success and failure are immaterial)
and your guarantee of lasting happiness, because you are
not looking outside yourself for the answers to life's
problems. Fear is as much an illusion as those things it
conjures up to prevent you from looking directly at the
true state, or reality.

Yellow is the colour of fear, of cowardliness; it is always
cringing and hiding but is never really able to escape from
being seen for what it is.

GRASPING
Greed, hatred and delusion are characterized in Buddhist

90 Melancholy: tree ivy and purple anemone against a black metal sculpture

teaching as the source of all suffering. The end to suffering is the extinction of these three, but this is not possible until you see this truth for yourself, and through your own experience, the why and the wherefore of this truth. Greed is grasping—reaching out for what you do not have, trying to hang on to what you do have, not only in the way of material possessions but also in the way of thoughts and feelings. It is sometimes very difficult to see that really to 'have' anything worth having, you must let go. This is especially true of what seem to be perfectly natural and positive emotions, such as the love of a parent for a child, and thoughts for its safety. But these, too, can bring suffering. Only by holding everything in the open palm of your hand do you really have it. This is a difficult distinction to understand, and once it is 'grasped' there is an end to grasping.

MELANCHOLY
Melancholy is the mood of self-absorption, of shutting

91 Caution: love-in-a-mist seed-heads and tulips with a piece of dried gnarled wood

yourself away with your own memories and the feelings, usually negative, that they evoke. It is a negation of the living world in preference for your own view of it, a vision coloured by sadness. As reality impinges, it seems to get entangled with these negative reactions and becomes distorted in such a way that it too can only be perceived as unhappy and unpleasant. The melancholy frame of mind is such a lonely one that it is hard to visualize anyone else wanting to associate with such a miserable member of the human race.

CAUTION

The word 'caution' implies a warning. You think of a yellow light in a traffic signal, or the flashing red light at the bend in the road. Take care, you are warned: watch what you are doing.

In the natural order of things, taking care is learning to understand and accept yourself as you are, not as an unchanging and unchangeable entity, but as a constantly

93 Joy: japonica and camellia
leaves, with freesia and driftwood in
the front container

evolving microcosm of nature. Exercising caution in this
context means being mindful and self-possessed in
everything you do. Your activity is not limited to outward
movement: you must take care in how you think and in
what you say. Throwing caution to the wind will only
create precisely the kinds of difficulties you are trying to
avoid. Then and only then you might learn the wisdom of
taking care. Here, it might be said that caution is the
better part of discretion.

ACCEPTANCE

Acceptance is the resolution of life's conflicts. This may
sound rather glib, but it is meant to be taken at a much
deeper level, for true acceptance is the acknowledge-
ment of the validity of both aspects of life: happiness
cannot exist without suffering, fullness without emptiness,
the dark without the light. Yet your everyday mind has a
way of resisting the acceptance of things as they are. You
wish often that things were different. In fact, by not

longing for the absence or the disappearance of whatever it is that you find disagreeable, by accepting everything, you find that the contentiousness that gives you anxiety and sleepless nights disappears.

JOY

Dr Suzuki often points out in his books on Zen Buddhism that the essential ingredients for the pursuit of enlightenment are great faith and great doubt. These appear to be contradictory, of course, but your aim is to bring them into balance so that they create a field of tension in which the activity of your search takes place. The emotional response to the realization of this state of balance can only be great joy. It is a kind of ecstasy which illuminates the whole personality and is as infectious as a baby's spontaneous smile. This great joy arises with the breaking of the bonds of delusion, the acceptance of everything as it is. It is sustained only as long as the tension between great doubt and great faith persists, as it indicates the attitude of liberation, not satisfaction at liberation having been achieved.

POETIC INSPIRATION

Alfred Koehn wrote one of the earliest books on ikebana for western readers, *The Art of Japanese Flower Arrangement*, published in 1933. In it he called ikebana poetry. 'It is to be regarded,' he said, 'rather as a means of giving expression to elevated ideas and as a method of suggesting hidden springs of culture, than as an actual interpretation of the beauties of nature. Its real purpose lies in the intangible; its true beauty is found in its symbolism of things incorporeal, in its suggestiveness and in its unfolding of veiled spirituality.' This statement could be applied throughout this book, to the seasonal arrangements as well as the philosophical themes and emotional moods. In what we see, it is what we do not actually see but is hinted at that gives the arrangement such power and depth. This is especially true when we come to poetry, above all the highly polished form of verse known as *haiku*. In seventeen Japanese syllables are condensed vivid and profound images.

I have already mentioned Reginald Blyth in the chapter on seasonal arrangements: I knew him when I was living in Japan. His four volumes on *haiku*, which are ordered according to the seasons, are invaluable for any arranger. Dr Blyth feels that the *haiku* is in itself an art of precision, a poem behind a poem in Mr Koehn's sense. He goes on to say, 'the unsaidness is the express attestation of the unsayableness that is part of the essential nature of poetry'.

In this final section I have chosen eight *haiku* and show them alongside the arrangements they inspired, so that you may experience the poem and its realization and then see what you can do yourself. (*For details of the arrangements see p. 168.*)

Sleet falling:
Fathomless, infinite
Loneliness

Joso

They spoke no word,
The host, the guest,
And the white chrysanthemum

Ryota

Autumn evening,
A crow perched
On a withered bough

Basho

157

The sea darkens;
The voices of the wild ducks
Are faintly white.

Basho

How wondrously supernatural,
And how miraculous this!
I draw water, I carry fuel!

P'ang-yun

The evening haze;
Thinking of past things,
How far-off they seem.

Kito

The old pond;
A frog jumps in:
The sound of water.

Basho

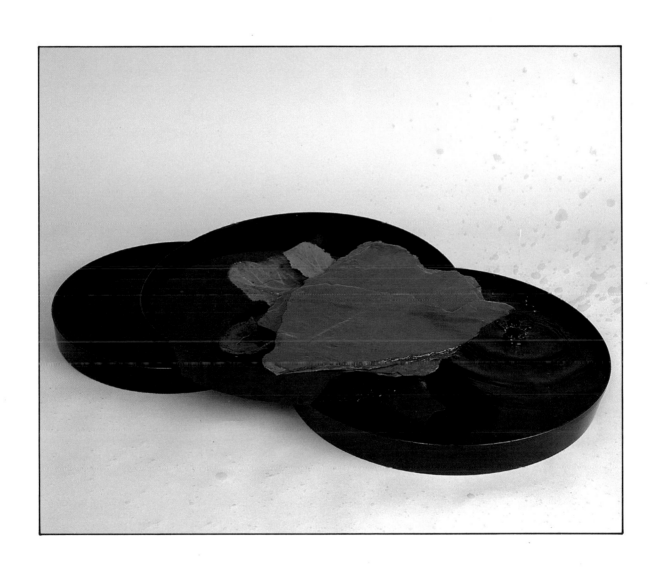

With the evening breeze
The water laps against
The heron's legs.

Buson

CONCLUSION

I hope this book has stimulated a desire in you, the reader, to practise the art of ikebana, whether you are a novice or have some experience of it. Maybe you have been leafing through it, going over particular arrangements or sections in a relaxed and easy way, taking up your *hasami* and setting out into the garden (or off to the florist's) on impulse. On the other hand you may have worked your way steadily through the book. In either case I would like to sum up the essential points once again. Throughout the book I have presented the basic arrangements in the sequence in which they should be studied – and I cannot stress the importance of this too strongly. They are so ordered that the student may approach the art with the simplest of arrangements and progress naturally and logically to those which require greater dexterity and deeper understanding. I think it is clear that there is much more to ikebana than the mere act of placing certain pieces in certain positions, and, as with any process of learning, the student should take it step by step if he or she is to reap its full benefits.

Through these pages I have emphasized that ikebana offers you a great deal in the way of pure personal pleasure and benefit, quite apart from its immediate aim of enhancing your surroundings. The joy of working creatively with flowers never diminishes, and it brings with it a sense of tranquillity and fulfilment. It offers complete relaxation, which to me is most important if you lead a busy and active life. For there is no feeling of competition in ikebana, no attempt to better someone else. The leading schools do not compete with each other, so neither should individual arrangers. The object is simply to create something of beauty for the delight of others and, in so doing, to improve yourself. And for what you are offered, you have something to offer in return. Every arrangement you make will be stamped with your individuality – uniquely and inimitably your personal contribution to an ancient and revered art.

It is my sincere wish that you gain as much enjoyment out of your ikebana as I have from mine.

GLOSSARY

Dai The wooden base upon which a container stands. An integral part of most arrangements in Japan, its use in the west is optional, but it does give a finished look to an arrangement as well as protecting the surface of furniture.

Hikae Literally translated as 'earth', it is the name given to the shortest of the three main stems in any Sogetsu School arrangement.

Ikebana Accepted as meaning 'flower arrangement', its literal translation is 'the arrangement of living plant material', and it is the general name given to all Japanese flower arrangement.

Ikenobo Literally translated as 'the temple by the lake', it is the name of the oldest school of flower arrangement in Japan.

Jushi The collective name for all material—flowers, branches, leaves or shrubs—used to supplement the main stems in any Sogetsu School arrangement.

Kakei Meaning 'one and one', it is the name given to a type of arrangement which uses only two main stems.

Kakemono A long, narrow, hanging picture, in the nature of a scroll, which complements the flower arrangement in a Japanese home.

Keishin-kei The general name given to arrangements which have an overall slanting or windswept appearance.

Kenzan Pinholder; this will already be familiar to western arrangers as the means of securing material in shallow containers.

Moribana Literally 'piled up'—the general name given to arrangements made in low, shallow containers.

Morimono The general name given to arrangements in which fruit and/or vegetables are combined with plant material.

Nageire The general name given to arrangements made in tall containers. Its literal translation is 'thrown in'.

Oyo Literally translated as 'style'.

Rikka Literally translated as 'standing plant cuttings', it was the name given to the massive arrangements that were the first to evolve in the history of Japanese flower arrangement.

Risshin-kei The general name given to arrangements which have an overall upright appearance.

Ryu Literally translated as 'school'.

Seika The symbolic triad of heaven, man and earth.

Shikibana An arrangement without a container, in a *kenzan*.

Shin Literally translated as 'heaven', it is the name given to the longest and most important of the three main stems in any Sogetsu School arrangement.

Soe Literally translated as 'man' (i.e. mankind), it is the name given to the secondary and medium-length stem of the three main stems in any Sogetsu School arrangement.

Tokonoma The recess in a Japanese room in which the flower arrangement stands.

Zokei Meaning 'changing of form', it is a general name applied to modern free style and abstract arrangements.

ACKNOWLEDGEMENTS

The author, the editor and John Calmann and Cooper Ltd would like to thank the following for their kind permission to use material from their books:

HOKUSEIDO PRESS for permission to quote from *Haiku*, Volumes II, III and IV by Reginald H. Blyth

ROUTLEDGE AND KEGAN PAUL for permission to quote from *The Art of Japanese Flower Arrangement* by Alfred Koehn

ELEMENT BOOKS for permission to quote from *The Heart of Religion* by Phiroz Mehta

RANDOM HOUSE INC. (Modern Library) for permission to quote from *The Wisdom of Lao-tse*, translated and edited by Lin Yutang

THE BUDDHIST SOCIETY for permission to quote from *The Field of Zen* by D. T. Suzuki

JOHN MURRAY LTD for permission to quote from *The Spirit of Zen* by Alan W. Watts

THAMES & HUDSON LTD and PANTHEON BOOKS, a division of Random House Inc., for permission to quote from *The Way of Zen* by Alan W. Watts

Thanks are also due to the ASHMOLEAN MUSEUM, Oxford, for permission to reproduce the illustrations in Plates 3, 7, 8 and 9

INDEX